MIRRORS MÁSCARAS

John M. Bennett

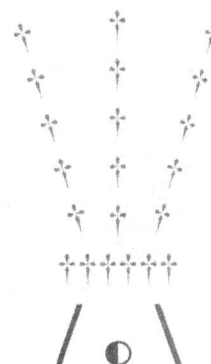

LUNA BISONTE PRODS
2014

MIRRORS MÁSCARAS
John M. Bennett

With love to C. Mehrl Bennett
For her Inspiration and Love

December 2012 - April 2013

Some of these poems have appeared in the following excellent publications: FLUXUS [audio LP]; Bizarre cities; Zeitzoo; Gritty Silk; Otoliths; Degu: A Journal of signs; 'Pider; Cricket Online Review; Hoak; Réparation de Poésie; Pense Aqui; Offerta Speciale; Open World; ReSite; On Barcelona; Truck; Big Hammer; Experiential-Experimental-Literature; Maintenant; Visual Poetry in the World; Altered Scale; Zombie Logic Review; Extreme Writing Community; Kart; Convocatoria de Poesía Visual Stop Desahucios; The Post-Literate (R)Evolution; Mail Art Makes the World a Town; Haiku Canada Review; and Blank Sight/Naked Sunfish.

And in the following chapbook and TLPs:
Algunos Mirrors, in, The Chapbook, 3, 2013.
Más Caras, Luna Bisonte Prods, 2012.
Máscaras del Tún, Luna Bisonte Prods, 2012.
Merienda Mortal, Luna Bisonte Prods, 2013.

Cover art by John M. Bennett; book design by C. Mehrl Bennett

ISBN 978-1-938521-13-3

LUNA BISONTE PRODS
137 Leland Ave.
Columbus, OH 43214 USA

http://www.lulu.com/spotlight/lunabisonteprods

Máscara del Ah

think
sodt *my pool my ash my*
cluster *lung my gnats my sit*
hole *my fog my plunge my*

äh *tab my wall my shirt*

seeping *my wallet my ash my*
phone *glue my runt my fell*

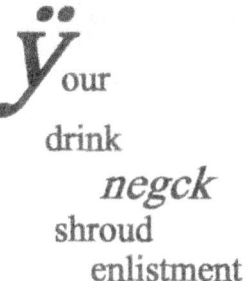

ÿour *my sore my tine my*

drink *stab my dringk my he*
negck *my plot my numb my*
shroud *gas my pill my tumbled*
enlistment

Máscara del Otro

elbow
slasher
pill
a knot a door a
shovel a pore a clot

O t
a wrist a tube a

her
table
burns
fold a corpse a sing
a dust a meal a
slot a mass a tool

inside
the barn
a mot a claw a
clanging a it a dot

not
thinking
drink
the shadows
a sweat a bee a
pillow a blue a foot

Máscara del Ojo

teeth
root *the feet the coin the*
half *ash the towel the too*

b◐ils *th**e** shore the dim the*
)crown the *nostril the ape the ton*
lake *the gate the crawl the*

ĝristle *sçissor the all the not*
falling *the sworn the pen the*
plaque ***boiling** the massive the is*
seething *the plunge the scrap the*
lung *plume the nates the bomb*
corn
aspirina(•

Máscara del Lint

flop
nest
cord *I mind I clod I*

nda *Upper I tot I shave*
slab *I rinse I at I*
burbuja *paw I you I knot*

Pantalón *i grant I haul I*
cagado *issue I came I tomb*
mortar *I fissure I it I ut*
mortal *ter I goad I nod*
size *I sweep an sleep I*
rabbit *fog I murmur I um*
lint.........

Máscara of the Bark

taste
of thread
hot cloud   *what it what was what*

*kn*ót   *cash what not what pill*
finger   *what hell what pile what*
slope   *flag what void what melt*

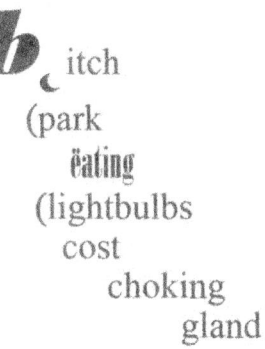

bc itch   *what gun what pull what*
(park   *meats what core what asp*
ëating   *irina what but what knock*
(lightbulbs   *what shade what if what*
cost   *bull what gag what frost*
choking
gland

Máscara de la Moneda

even~~
ink~
gland *o fog o meal o*

cRack *newt o god o plan*

stubble *o dud o mile o*
nekkid *mute o lung o mite*
slug *o fig o clam o*

d,ander *egg o dent o shore*

(plot *o crap o blot o*
)cough *burger o nap o gnat*
(window *o scald o sheet o*
lapse *blade o smell o dime*
burnt
shades

Máscara Ciega

Long~~~~~~~~~~

Lapsed~~~~~~~

Leg~~~~~~ *no thong no trash no*

ĝunner *seal no rice no log*

shaped *no dice no big no*

by h ash *hammer no butt no ice*

≈drizzle *no fool no hit no*

oosmosist **ch***ewer no awe no mite*

tell me *no nit no crash no*

(desierto *armpit no heel no mute*

thud ***no boil*** *no dung no*

(gland wind *lot no dust no wall*

crust of *no tube no glottis no*

bushes *raw no rug no explanat*

~burnt *ion*

~sticks —— ——

Máscara del Silencio

dog
and fail
≈sleep≈ *nod off nod pool nod*

atl *Sponge nod hand nod it*

≈blood≈ *nod clown nod runt nod*
door *plot nod shun nod lore*
leaks *nod dole nod blaster nod*
er gotten *pen nod dunk nod limb*

ëndend **NO***d pus nod loot nod*

ok with *boil nod lamp nod tore*
Clanking *nod kelp nod trunk nod*
earlobe ***ándale*** *nod dot nod not*
Crossing *nod buzz nod toil nod*
list of *double nod daub nod trance*
howlers *nod lawn nod lock nod*
smattered *bubbling bubbling*
porn
er~ ~ ~ ~ ~ ~

Máscara of the Seen

toss ‘ ‘ ‘ ‘
hack
the blear *and wind and sock and*

Viento *thr**oa**t and vine and itch*

risible *and growl and wham and*
ni modo *deck and knive and snore*

»los ojos ***an**d lip and thorn and*
tumbales *smoke and file and drain*
((chile *and ant and bale and*
hormigón *fire and wheel and grope*
((gusano *and chain and sand and*
inevit*a* *plop and soak and heal*
“*ble* ary” *and dog and sleep and*
(cut it *door and pile and ends*
off / / / ___

Máscara of the Cracks

l l ll l lllll l ll *the* l l lllll l llll l l

un listed dog whole slab
chewed beneath the table gr

itty sausage fauce*t t* ime your c

rawling h**O** wl ladder l***O*** ot lint

fell outside the combed hair litter tr

aced inside your f**OG** ged literacy
rate of dogfood smeared across the
lawn your *FLAGLESS* neck s
ear your dunkel bag d
ropped onto the d
riveway
†
†
†
†
†
††††††

Máscara Mojada

heat the ~ ~ ~ ~ ~
ladder lint ·· ·· ·· ·· ·· ··
the stinking *clown wave ice wave peel*

fÖam *wÄve dog wave elbow wave*

blistered *bill wave vain wave shine*
ham *wave cloud wave hill wave*
blend *sandwich wave she wave corner*

On yr *wave blood wave dry wave*
chin *sit wave fart wave master*
(stings *wave ball wave shorts wave*

boat *steam wave indoor wave clad*
(sinking *wave mute wave chatty wave*
sunlight *seen wave lost wave bloat*
on white *wave idiot wave plunder wave*
islands ≈ ≈ ≈ ≈ ≈ ≈ ≈ ≈≈ ≈

Máscara Cagada

aäaaä ã aäaaä
sticky shorts drying in the
wind your my impactor grinding

≈≈toward àhalt" beáns burb≈≈
ling in "what" intestino's shape

ly thigh fasts Andado como dr

~~~ifting ape ,fea●●thered hallway~~~
where your clicking wrist knew
my clot ***(NOTHING)*** hot wit
h random mood and
sizzled shad ow
in the bath
room

/ ◐ \
~~~

Máscara of the Guest Check

for Jim Leftwich

fish≈

\slab of/

~lung hair claw~

~mic è sit shóe bor~

e ham hill leaks bled d

irt cloud lin•t door him

~~blast ink bag holes gun~~

eye loose mot anda lay dus

t shawl HOG ICE lump dim

~e tool brack dink~

~mule rust~

~comb~

c

H

i

x

Máscara de los Setenta

~~~*7Õ*~~~

thumbs 70 *smear*

70 *necks* floating in

the lake 70 turds 70 cash ha

~~mmers 7**Ò** lucks 7õ pizzles~~

70 suitcases 70 dog breaths 70 teeth

70 jars of rain 70 **o7** sandwiches drib

~~~bling on your 70 laps 70 chairs with~~~

71 sticky skulls *7070707* rooms stuffed

with *búrning pápér* 70 sk

inned washers their eyes bl

~~~inking in the 70 base~~~

~~ments where my~~

~70 fog wrassles~

~with your 70~

~stinking~

~**bones**~

~õ~

o
~~~

Máscara Evolutiva

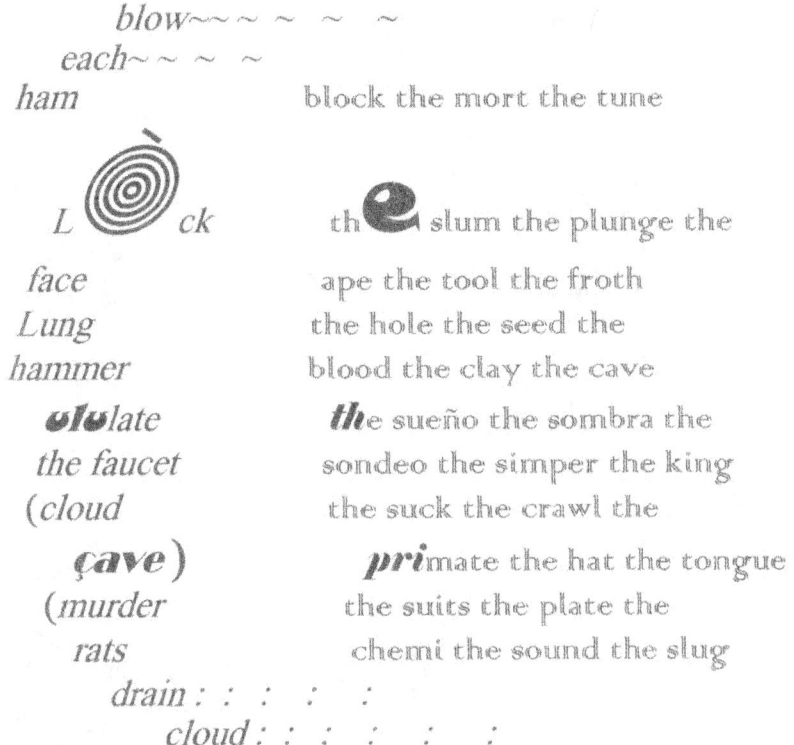

blow~~ ~ ~ ~ ~
each~ ~ ~ ~
ham block the mort the tune

Lòck the slum the plunge the

face ape the tool the froth
Lung the hole the seed the
hammer blood the clay the cave
ululate the sueño the sombra the
the faucet sondeo the simper the king
(cloud the suck the crawl the
çave) **pri**mate the hat the tongue
(murder the suits the plate the
rats chemi the sound the slug
drain : : : : :
cloud : : : : : :

Máscara del Espejo

thé *uh uh uh uh uh uh*
sock *uh uh uh uh uh*
the *plunged into my sweaty*
sÕle *thunder blanket hot*
the *with drugs and halitosis*
stung *songster crawling toward the*
the *pillow where your ants re*
b,lade *tained the leaking of my*
OOthe *aspirinaspiration soap and*
young *wheels ,logs and towers ,fog*
the *cornered in a skull collapsing*
(gag *dog hovel beaded with the*
the *rain my towels forgot*
(soap *to swing beside the windy*
the *corner where your shovels*
mute *rust and shine outside the night*
the & & & & &
scrawl & & & & & &

Máscara Mútua

mantis
soap *la*
•pinhead *sombra lamida la*
Ojo **ca***ja investida de la*
y mis *tumba tronada la*
cojones *vestimenta ovalada la*
Cuadrados *puerta ventosa la*
los cinco ***su****tura lívida la*
(**sentidos** *manta inmiscerable la*
insect ***com****ida fonética la*
(**ívoros** *sarna literaria la*
que me *comisura de la llaga la*
comían *pestilencia olvidada*
los *la*
párpados

Máscara de la Luz Oscura

~~~ñ ñ ñ és ñ ñ ñ ñ~~~
~~pejo destinado es~~
~lumbre ahogada es~
la tuerca del ojo later
al es onda a dobado es
tripa deletreada es el mamo
~treto fiscal es soMbra es o suertudo~
es el poniente FriSado de tus nalg
as es lo pormenor de mi por may
or es no ES ENENCIA es luna
~~≈es formicona es cuarzo≈~~
~≈liberado y caca es ,com≈~
~≈ejón y luz bajo≈~
~≈la tierra≈~
≈o≈
~ō~
o
o
o
o
0o0
~~~

Máscara del Cumbre

or my~~~~~~~~~~~
ticker~~~~~~~~~
mutters~~ *eat ice eat snore eat*

(i**ñ**) (**thé**) ***(ca)(ge)*** *eat nostril eat blow*
laundry *eat inch eat tool eat*
chute *ash eat rose eat climb*
your *eat spill eat shorts eat*
*F*aucet cl *mister eat skim eat day*
oud ***ea****t hash hair eat mold eat*
dampness *cash eat mule eat drink*
(thought *eat brim eat neck eat*
sky~ *hole eat nude eat grave*
(lumbers *eat issue eat mud eat*
toward *cream eat noose eat it*
~~the *eat tongue eat eye eat*
~~meatless *thins............*
~~cliff

Máscara Chihuahuense

•\\\\\\\\\nor *T* eño/////////•
~~a pesar del lodo a pesar del~~
hombre inmantado a pesar del del
~ta del tezontl **è** del po **é** ma arraiga~
do en el amate en **Â** scua tripartita a
pesar de la nube ofidiosa de lo dicho p
~~≈or la nuca ,nunca olvidriosa nunca si≈~~
(empre a pesar de lo **(GRUÑIDO)** a pesar de la)
selva en el fondo de tu garganta a pesar
de la barca perdida por los veri
~~≈cuetos de la ciénaga diseca≈~~
~≈da por el sendero in≈~
~≈infinito hacia el≈~
~≈su sur≈~

o
&
&
&
&
&
==&==

Máscara of the Mask

~

~~usher~~
~~out the s~~
~~~torm wobble~~~

,,lucrÖ̃ Över,,
past the sand
which Ŧable ¿w
here's supper? spl
~~≈ashed fingers at yr≈~~
•)outlet ***(VALVE)*** twist(•
ed off the wall s
≈pent thunder≈
≈dogs twitch≈
~ing~
§
§
§
§
§
~~wind~~
~~~

Máscara Ladrante

,,,*diêntes* tlhle *diêntes*,,,,

~blender dog cashed~
~~inmondado kites my~~
~~~hash wiggled in your~~~
⁂sleep Òvulatiõn sciss⁂
or it's lo asumiso o el rin
cón imbuído de ,Ñudo fatigado
,rumbo inflado ,oscilante ,rajado
,,,,,teeth crashing on the hair-wrapped,,,,
)blades o **(PISONTE)** "twitching"(
in the sheets your creamed
~~corn shorts your run~~
~~ny beard soaked~~
~~~into the p~~~
i
i
l
l
l
≈*ow*≈

Máscara de Calabaza

~~~skull HÁLF suit~~~
~~the meat I wore beneath~~
~~~my skin jumpy steak wind~~~
~ow al reflejÖ al reflujÕ wh~
ere I was mirrored but was not was gl
≈≈)aring blindly at a sT one burning on(≈≈
the driveway carretëra inmóvil ,vena
viscosa faster than my thought rever
sal sputter ed in (THE CLOUD)y bat
≈hroom door that)soap I wore(≈
≈)*the sticky blood strea*(≈
≈)*king down my leg*(≈
≈♦≈
♦
♦
♦
♦
♦
s.e.e.d.s

Máscara de Mesa

~~*beast* “the” *lunch*~~
~table with that fog be~
~neath your chewing sock et~
•hereal spÒnge en tÛcogote•
¿what dilution’s this what drumm
ing neck desfoco deshógarado ahog
~~≈ado como sweat,,,,,,,,,,,,,,,,,,,pooling in≈~~
~≈your hat what? **)“change”(** is “ne≈~
~≈ver”( )*ever siempre es ,y en≈~*
≈tu manantial de caca está≈
e
s
t
a
p
a
~*.do.*~

Máscara del Mohín

~~~ne b l í na~~~

~~lapsus con)las plumas~~
~~circulares y el aire de mi~~
~~culo antro vaivuelve vuelviva~~

..]door way d ormido[b olver y no..

,bolver)intento(Â o de colgar reres

tivo ,raquítica tu Ü ña rumorífica de
tu vapor tento //////\\\\\\ )*shadowed list*(
,shredding in the **(DUST'S)** a mueca olvid,
≈≈osa que mis huesos osan ,inmiscible≈≈
≈≈en la carne vácua en mi≈≈
≈≈s alas "en el cielo"≈≈
≈*gris*≈

::
::
::
::
::
::

....:●:....
~~~

Máscara de la Hoja

......,*the* duSTy *the*,.....

.....,socks the snake,.....
........,the lens the date the,........

,,,emanåtion thêgun the co,,,

mb sandwich The shot luggage

the scam the pl,U,nge the neck the
≈llamamama the ***s,o,a,k,i,n,g*** the trudged flat≈
((scoria clattering ***(DOWN THE)*** slope shattered))
wall and your screamy boots fin
,,,,,,,ally sinking in the gritty va,,,,,,,
,,,,,,lley where the clock the,,,,,,
,,,,,gate *the dense face's,,,,,*
,,,,revelation's one,,,,
,,,and torn,,,
/
\
/
\
/
\
\ ,■, /

Máscara of the Waves

sla**b**≈≈≈≈≈≈≈≈≈≈≈≈≈≈≈≈≈≈≈≈

the focus≈≈≈≈≈≈≈≈≈≈≈≈

net *what hash what putrifaction what*
~shirt *issue what stubble what throat*

ghost **wh***at illumination what itch what*
~spinning *choking what drain what glutination*
past the *what asks what burns what*
cave *mustard what dick what glass*

Od**O**r w**ha***t pocket what offal what's*
b,l,a,z,i,n,g *heard what mute what whines*
(hotdog *what bend what it's what*
ON THE SILL ***shal****low what swallow what was*
(stone *what tomb what lens what*
cold *hollow what fly what yes*
buttons *what bore what fume what's*
in yr *ondaemética*≈≈≈
ear

‘ ‘ ‘ ‘ ‘

Máscara del Lago

~~thé ó ó ó ó ó ó ó
~~bréaded o o o o o
~lake *wet gun wet ass wet*
your *plate wet door wet watch*
Licking *wet fog wet noose wet*

LIP *wind wet belt wet mime*
~shore *wet list wet pill wet mine*
feathers *wet hill wet speech wet*
cloudy *undulation wet mot wet mail*
b.ottles *wet turds wet loaf wet*
gr ave l *temple wet ounce wet dug*
my shattered *wet fold wet sleep wet*
(knee *lock wet grin wet boil*
STRINGY ***wet** cheeseburger wet gnat wet*
(muscle *table wet neck wet crime*
streaming *wet nickel wet thumb wet*
≈in the *closet wet moon wet reticulation*
≈back
≈flow

Máscara Cantada

~sssss bél'ts sssss~
~~singer spout singer shut singer~~
~~plaid singer plod singer ape singer it's~~
~~singer fog singer bland singer knife singer~~

...flab singër dro Ól singer dual..

singer pour singer M•orph singer dork
~~≈singer fall singer putz singer flat≈~~
(singer (ÇLOUD SINGER) rat singer)
porch singer blood singer nightmare
≈singer halt singer op≈
≈singer bulb singer≈
≈blinding singer≈
~s~
s
s
s
s
~~rinSég~~

Máscara Punto Final

thé lush /ſſſ//ſſſ/// / ſ / . . . .

lunch
~~loot

/Œst~

~~)inches(
hissing
in your
Sandwich

μndulante
(fog and
CHOPPING
(gristle
twitching
~in the
~sticky
~dust . . . .
,
,
,
,
,

lo uso la asa el oso lo
muerto el viento la cumbre

el tÚnel la manga el fin la
tapa en tuerto lo simple
el sueño lo súper la puerta ni
núbil in farto la boca
el dedo lo lento la pasta no
pUlcra lo sumo el rumbo
la bolsa el fusil la mano tu
DIEnte lo mudo el polvo
la ronda el norte la tuerca lo
singular la lluvia el primero
y último lo múltimo

Máscara de l'Eau in Flames

~~~~in Ç re~~~~
~~~de ma visage d'acide~~~
~~~formique)*chasing the nest*(~~~

.)nubes y Ojos(la flatUlencia ri.
sueña ,"druggy")*shade*(cloggin
g the cloud of (p)(o)cket lint)lo es
crito en llamas ,andantes las ,hojas esfé
,ricas ,piedras (CUADRADAS) ni ,oscul,
.antes ,le lac oublié y te es.
≈≈cucho ,mano ,te ed≈≈
≈ito ,*tus palab*≈
≈*abradas li*≈
≈*ke ash*≈
≈ ; ≈
;
;
;
≈≈;≈≈
~~~

Máscara de la Jaqueca

~~èhèhèhèhreÀehúhúhúhúh~~

~~~*ambulition squelching in the mud* my~~~

~~~~gorra de tezontle's ***tarry smoke's*** the fr~~~~

==:ame do G my thou**g**ht aggregate:==

's)shrinking blac**K**• hole fog or towel's

itch gate spellin**g** **a**t your puls ing ne

>>}ck¡ ah spinning suit what named my{<<

face !my corn (**HEAVING**) in your

sotintestinano)¡ay si sangrara!(

≈≈≈mas los mocos los tienen va≈≈≈

≈≈cíos vacíos los lentes *y*≈≈

≈≈*en la boca tu na*≈≈

≈≈*da mora*≈≈

≈≈oo≈≈

oo

oo

oo

oo

oo

oo

~∞òó∞~

•

Máscara de la Carroña

émbólísmó∞∞∞∞∞∞∞∞∞∞∞

●fratricidio∞∞∞∞∞∞∞∞∞∞

estornudo *si tinta si mudo si*

hórnó *fuego si erre si loco*

Õmbligante *sî boli si mamo si*

mis tunas *frunço si llama si peldaño*

sin es *si mono si taco si*

pinazo *hormiga si nada si calzado*

,**P**,●co **SI** *asno si lentes si*

dicen *chomba si ronda si asta*

(mas la *(si ego si goma si*

Logorrea ***lap**so si pàgina si ipso*

(pleno el *(si acto si lomo si*

~lunar *fonética si herida si tor*

~~central *bellino si bolsa si brazos*

~~~de lo *putrefactos*

~~~~impensable

Máscara Muy Mojada

....rrrrru Ŧ ílanteeeee....
....huevo de mirasol un cuento....

soy que c Ü enta el □́ tro ,él

que nunca habla)µ(like a bowl of (s
oup)(the forgottten dock where the
~~grey ship clanked and groaned wh~~
ere the scribbled (P.L.O.T) se)*perdió*
por el mar(💧)soaked in el dribbling
~~sea)*de hamburguesas lleno*((~~
~~de tonadas iimmbbéécciilleess~~
~~)que me contaban todo lo~~
~~que no sé de la~~
~~nada donde~~
~nado~
💧
💧
💧
💧
💧
💧
💧
💧
≈≈💧≈≈(

Máscara del Desayuno

ééxxéndémico~~
lo preto~~
pulmónico
~flaca fraca

..................Ûbre

~fangoso
y mi trono
cajas

C,agadas
ölas
amigadas
(desayuno
RECORDADO
(como brisa
flag r
ante
el reloj
≈de los

≈sangüiches,
‘
‘
‘
‘

toast nor flood nor ate
nor lip nor leg nor

acrid nor is nor itch

nor tube nor floor nor
pile nor steam nor fail
nor run nor cough nor

grime nor as nor was
nor wrench nor dust nor
wave nor putresence nor he
(nor done nor gate nor
DRY *nor fog nor peel*
(nor wheat nor egg nor
gag nor clock nor lake
nor blood nor lisp nor
think nor loud nor biting down

Máscara of the Freezer

thunder≈≈≈ ≈ ≈ ≈ ≈ ≈ ≈

ash~ *what eye what boil what*

~*l*oop the sh *~shoe what door what word*

Út **W***hat thought what pin what*

~hot *~block what dark what street*

lunch *what cracked what plate what*

hash *bleeding what tongue what sore*

•**F**,,oiled **W***hat flood what wind what*

~hair~ *gaze what glass what sliver*

(wet *(what blind what as what*

BU.T.TS **BAT** *what knew what told*

(dry *(what wallet what guano what*

crickets *plunge what ask what neck*

~legs *~what blade what out what*

~broke *~smell what fence what stop*

~off ~ ~~ ~~~ ~~~~

ㄴ
ㄴ
ㄴ
ㄴ
ㄴ
ㄴ
ㄴ

Máscara de la Luz Quebrada

~~iñmi ÑËñcia~~

~~~tu foco estrellado~~~
~~~~tus lentes de lodo lamido~~~~

.....tu desaf © co fictur ã tivo des.......

OhechoOcomoOlunaOfátuaO *elObiO*

.........sonte en la cue V *a dormido es..........*

un hecho rehecho ,,,,,,,,,,,, rememoriado e

histerórico es lo (**pünzànte**) gasa
lcohólico de tu melancalcomanía
~~~~tus recueldos como rescoldos~~~~
~~~tus lapsos que son ojos~~~
~~y tus formas anta~~
~gónicas que~
~son polv~
~os y~
v
e
n
t
i
s
c
~~*o*~~
~~~*s*~~~
~~~

Máscara of the Loot

talk's;;;; ;;; ;; ; ; ; ;
Loot *ach mind ach wind ach*
Leak *dorm ach ant ach left*
~~Loot *ach boom ach neck ach*

F lat **sh***ape ach lock ach play*

Loot *ach shore ach dark ach*
snore *heel ach nods ach time*
Loot *ach loot ach seal ach*
Less *bloat ach ling ach lung*

L ooot **ac***h soot ach plot ach*

dollop *nest ach deed ach done*
(Loot *ach olvido ach hymn ach*
FLUNG$ ***spray*** *ach gear ach sink*
(Loot *ach toe ach cramp ach*
~~peels *blade ach spout ach seems*
~~Loot
t
t
t
t
t
t
t
t............

Máscara Lodesca

" ' , ' " ' ' " ' ' " '

~~èwchè W C héwch~~

~~~black slaw the mute mort the~~~
~~~~mot mist muttering behind the~~~~

,garag è ,my sm Õ ke plate under,

your chair the F rying words stiffen
in my freezing breath's outer cl
••oud ay the (M.AT.ERM.U.D) rises at•
the door your shadowed leg suit
grins my marbled jaw
≈≈≈≈my collar fog my≈≈≈≈
≈≈≈lunch water≈≈≈
≈≈gagging≈≈
≈at≈
th
e
m
i
r
r.o.r

Máscara Meriendal

~bomb the ham✈✈✈✈ ✈ ✈ ✈ ✈
~bomb the corn sweating in my s
~~neck bomb miling lap reduction of

th **é** *lake* **a**ir falling from your face

bomb the watched the gnats cloud a
grease cross the street a skull
bomb flickers in the air YOUR LEG

t,he toilet *A*CROSS THE GRASS une cal
bomb the idgramme un choclo wet with
(coiled rat (memory of ,window writ with
B.O.M.B *the* ***ash*** pills streaked across
(boiling (the light a sandwich
cloud QUIVERS IN THE CORNER
bomb the
acetaminophin

Máscara de la Cama

≈the
≈the shirt apt to boiling ,in your cacophone
≈the sheet ,index *spilling down the stairs* ,wh
≈the shot y occupation of the shovelled s
≈≈the shift kin *remembered in the hole* a

thëshoot lõt strewn with pillows and

the shoe ,fog pulsing down the block my
the shame acrid squirrel "thinking" apt t
the shore o ,*fistulent* ,its sticky carpet

.the shout stinks beneath the bed .apt to

the,,,,,,,,sham was ,of finger lessened ,was ,a
(the shawl (lesson *how to love the spade*
***the* SHU.T** :your door was open and the
(the shudder (screen your breath was rusted
the sheer *like a spoon* saying what you
the shit never said but FINISHED ON
the shadow THE BURNING BLANKET
the
ʃʃʃʃʃʃʃʃʃʃʃʃ
O

Máscara del Alba

my lúnç*h*~..~....~.. . . .
soake*d* *name* the sock the
~glan*d* *dog the rice the blade*

èvaporatio*n* *th***é** *sunset the dropping*

~coughin*g* *wind the shirt the toaster*
up th*e* *clicking in the afternoon the pore*
spoo*n* *the drying hand the winged*

e, Xhumatio*n* ***St****reetlamp the shoe speaking*
wher*e* *of elections the reddened*

(the wheezin*g* *(snore the barking on the*
FL,OO,R *'s* ***ROOF*** *the grassy handrails*

(stunne*d* *(the fountain covered~*
~~shin*y* *with hats and~~*
~~~wit*h* *moths~~~*
~~~~swea*t* *h*
o *s*
o *h*
o *s*
o *h*
s**O**s

Máscara de los Espejos

_._._ÀlbÁ._._._

~~~bestial ,congoja~~~
~~ventanal de sierras let~~
~radas mis plumas no vuelan~
~,escritãs ,afÓnicas trem~
bling ,in the base,**M**,ent of your j
≈aw tu garganta ,instigante ,man≈
guera ***(V,ER,DE,)*** en nudos ar
ξξtefactficiales ,azul con laξξ
ξξtarde invisible *.enξξ*
ξun barrio distanteξ
✪*algO se*✪

c x
a p
e l
o
c d
e e
s
~~~

Máscara del Pollo

~~k~k~k~*thé s*~k~k~k~~
~~kinned air~~
~~sheet folder dreamed~~
~~where yr turkey sandwich~~

≈*vapor* **I** *mpens* **á** *ble*)downed≈

~the shadowed ≈f**ÖR**k≈)I shivered next~
your cor,,,pse((*le faim inpisible* but the
≈drain was ,(**STARVING**) ,buried por≈
●la sábana was yr memobrane lea●●
☙kly counted mas inumesable in❧
☙ombrable inadadable *comme une*❧
☙*chose* clucking like your❧
☙chicken❧
☙kl❧
kl
kl
kl
∞***kl***∞

Máscara Cuadrada

nòr yòùr blòck hálf wístlés knéé
the tundrandom yr shaker suck
nor ape cuadrado swelling next
the folde**d** soup you**r** SH IRT
G LISTENS w**hë** n the slope
danced its rain and running leav
es pirante (**FLAVOR**) of
your HAND plunged into the
boiled bolsillo you were canto
inca ntado drinking off your si ≈≈

≈lent≈

r

O

a

r

Máscara Vicenteana

boil the≈" "≈≈ "≈≈≈' ' ' ' ' '
lint list a≈≈ '≈≈≈' ' '≈' ' ' ' ' '
~way ma tombent mis caras

t **ê** *te* **to**mbent mis lentes t

~s'éloigne ombent mis pies tomben
de ma t mis llagas tombent mi

C*orps e* **s p**eines tombent las nub
the wet es tombent mes yeux tom
(roof speeds (bent mis túneles tombent
ch'e've'lur'e ***mis*** lagos tombent mis
(the dust (boletos tombent mis co
is lost pihues tombent mis *haches*
≈ my clown tombent mis llaves tomb
≈ my neck ent mis dedos sur les
≈ un pont cercles
≈ qui o
≈ tremble≈ o
[más allá del o
Horizon Carré] O
O

Máscara de la Huaca

~~ ● ~~

∂ piedra de hueso ∂
∂ piedra de lucro pie ∂
∂ dra♦ de las luces del va ∂

~~lle diS'tante pie•Dra de~~

~los labios piedR♦a de lenkgua~

piedra futilesca que cae en la
calle piedra (,*callada*,) piedra
del pulmón piedra del ácido
goteante de la cara piedra si
~~miesca piedra ventanal pied~~
~~ra rumorífica del sueño~~
~~inti mista escondida~~
~~en la cueva cir~~
~~cular de mis~~
~◐~
j
◐
s
(*cl.o.s.ed*)

Máscara del Silencioo

-for C. Mehrl Bennett

la jaula de ▣◘⊡◈◘▪▪⊡≈

laundry la ▣□◇◘≈

~~jaula de libros   chased my sticky pants

o....................*l***ã.** *jaula*   **á**cross the steamy par

~~de linty   king lot the beercans

forks la   full of light rolling from the

jaula de   hissing wheels the ticking

window   in my left ear skeeter's

g,*lass la*   **S**hort skreeks the right

jaula de   *on the edge a falling tree*

(John la   (**coins** murmur in my pock

J/A/U/L/A   ***et*** ,just ahead ,cuffs

(del dentifricio   (**slapping** asphalt ,shoes

la jaula   forgotten ,coughing in

~of legs la   the bushes rustling

~jaula del   through the after

~aire muy   noon

~visible   n

n

n

n

n

i

◎

Máscara of the Gnat

≈≈≈dr*i*nk≈≈≈

≈≈the shadow lib≈≈
≈snoration in your≈
~~linty nose the clock's~~

~dim h **Ù** m dim h **Ú**m a~

cross the e**M**pty room
a gnat resting on your knee
this is nothing where the light
you finger (silence) chewed
off the book for years &
slumped into the ash
windowed in yr
~fire~
p
l
a
c
e

Máscara of the Laundry

my.,..léégg'sS≈≈.≈≈≈..≈≈,≈≈≈≈..≈

choking	*mumbling laundry gravel*
mist's	*in the laundry ice and shit*
≈*dim teeth*	*the laundry laundry damper*
y Õ ur	*lOaf hidden in the laundry*
≈swallowed	*where my laundry whistles*
face	*like a blank screen the laundry*
folded	*imposition on a Thursday*
flag	*slept beside the yearly laundry*
lentils	*wore my suit of laundry*
(dribbling	*(centered in a cloud of*
,,,,,,,,,,,,,,,,long	*sticky lint my laundry*
(down	*(mouth was shut was*
my	*d r y y*
chin	

o

o

o

o

O

oooooo

Máscara del Rábano

'R'

ɞ∂rábānō∂ɞ

ɞde mente rábanoɞ

ɞɞinilustrado rábano oɞɞ

ɞɞɞfOcO infértil O fértilɞɞɞ

,• *como* P *iédrá li,* T *érál* ráb...

ano al borde De mi lago in

≈≈≈≈textinal o rábano retorç≈≈≈≈

o~~~~~~~ido ,(*explicåtivo*) del porqué~

de mis **comidas** comailonas

;;;;;;rábanos aseverados rábanos;;;;;;

;;;;;insoñados dormidos des;;;;;

;;;;pertativos como;;;;

;;;futres y fangos;;;

;;sin;;

b

◎

a

aaa

Máscara Vácua

ï

~olÏVes~

....thunder the plate.....

.......*my flat face glistens*.......

.......)separ ation ¢loud ,nöstril(.......

~~where the foot dranK off where~~

)*lïpòpäct~iòn*( )*fóg väc úh*(

♒♒“chEEsy” illuMination of the♒♒

💧sandwich sweating in your “future”💧💧

≈≈≈paw the *(streaming)* picture gate’s≈≈≈

≈≈smouldered hinges where≈≈

≈*where you* lungched≈

≈*into the world*≈

≈v≈

o

i

d≈

Máscara of the Fire

~*snore* ~~ ~~ ~~ ~~ ~~ ~~
~leaving≈≈≈≈ ≈≈≈ ≈≈ ≈ ≈
~*my snake* so fought so beet so
≈brig *ggggg* glassy so thin so fault

,,,,,,,,,,,,,,,,,, Gásoline So noose so stink so
≈.amplify wobbled so ran so shirt
the b so cut so soot so
Linking spurting so glim so mer
Laundry so nostril so damn so
B, *urning* Never so was so *blearnt*
íñ thé ýárd so slept so walked so
(toss my (mumbled so dripped so wheel
*idddddddddddddddd***doll head** *so mute* so nattered so
(on the fire (blurbling so numbed so rock
water so peel so rot so
creeping flagged so meats so dry so
toward so
your shoe s
e s
e s
e o
e S
end

Máscara do Bandeirante

~m↗y tímé,,,,,,,

~múst,,,,,,,,

~bóré damp flag my swall

≈the aft owed flag neck twi

eeeeeeeeeeeeeeee **ê**rbirth **S**ted worm flag sheet

≈*SWIRLS* flag shirt flag sheet

IN THE JET flag shirt soaking in

TRAILS the cornflakes flag gun

U,lulation **F**ALLING FROM THE WINDOW

in your flag shorts you chew flag

coffe•e knot flag lip flag inch

_kkkkkkkkkkkkkkkkkkkkkk t.i.c..k.i.n.g *throaty* dimunition flag

IN YOUR hall burning poles lean

HAND against the horizon flag

~was fog nodder flag amputation

~was•ink BLEEDING ON THE

~*spreading* CONCRETE

~*in the laundry* e

i e

i e

Máscara of the Flood

≈≈mèatlàké≈≈
≈≈risen *shoe* flood≈≈
≈≈≈the walls dissolve the≈≈≈
"[RAKE SINKING IN YOUR"

,,,,,,*MUD* the T hroat ha**S**h regurg,,,,,,

libation spattere**d**,,**Ö**n the though
tless lunch a dog drowning down
≈≈≈the block *your fing er strokes*≈≈≈
my fac e (**C,HEW,ING,**) water and
≈≈*THE BEND ⓞF TIME* clotted≈≈
≈≈earwax slippers fil≈≈
≈led with rocks≈
≈a shining≈
≈**C**≈
a
m
b
~ ΠΠ ~

Máscara del Pozo

*dróó*ping ín thé b r é é z é , , , , ,
"en un pozo" ⊙
chewed the
~gland flag

⚐⚐⚐⚐⚐⚐ **d**amp

spongy
wheeze

t.he clock

~⊗⊗⊗⊗
(the circled
.◷◷◷◷◷◷◷ ***sky***
(dims
THE LAST
LINE OF
BIRDS
gone
♈
♈
♈
♈
♈
♈
♈

...de que dos Indios
miserables que por un

Corto interés entraron

en un pozo á limpiarlo,
fueron sofocados con el

pestilente vapor que

exhalaba... Gazeta de
(México del Martes 17 de

Junio de 1788

(Matehuala, where the
sun came up where
the shoes were
worn
r
r
r
r
r
r

Máscara dei Pasti

≈éã *t*ér≈

≈≈at the lake≈≈
≈≈≈*glistens and grey*≈≈≈
volcán▲▲ de sombra ▲▲ inmime

,nsa la **Õ** rilla‿distântë **É** *n una,*

piedra pensé ,**ín**v**í**sible ,en
≈las aguas somewhere hides ,el≈
fin de (**PAJA**,) que me espera
espero ,plato de *tallarines* y
≈≈≈aceite ,sliding off my≈≈≈
≈≈lap the *lliquidd legss*≈≈
≈draining,, , from my≈
≈pants≈
S
L
L
L
L
≈**L**•≈

Máscara of the Silt

≈≈.th*I*nk≈≈

≈≈≈lake§hair≈≈≈
≈≈≈≈your soap glass≈≈≈≈
)*foamy gun*(the stro
),,lling Çorner,,,,of yr,,,m,**ou**th,(

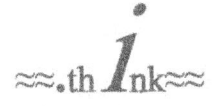

........)my ssuu8,gaarr my(*g*guullet........

.......drift an walll¨llls of *clcl*.......
ououdd)shouldered suits *sh(*
~redded in the **(boiling grass)** gro~
pe the **muudd** yr watch fills with

...... ssilt fissh∞q*ui*ver in th*e*......

.....*§§§§*w*ee*ds*§§§§*.....
§ s §
§ *d*
e
e
§*w*§§

Máscara of the Bullet

~tímë í í í

~tooth▲≈ ≈ ≈ ≈

~rõõõt leaf gristle bare gris

~~fórked tle chair gristle wiggler

oooooooooooooo è yebull Gristle lung gristle sand

~slaw a wich gristle speed gristle

head sock gristle tongue gristle egg

dribbler gristle loud gristle moan gr

B @ullet istle lube gristle phone gri

shaped stle ape gristle flag gristle

(but bit (dud gristle nope gristle af

aaaaaaaaaaaaaa T|HE| A|IR TER gristle lead gristle

(off its (god gristle 4 o'clock grist

≈neck le aim gristle grave g

≈stump ristle butt gristle

≈≈spouting i

≈≈≈rain i

i i

i i

i i

i S

i

n

Máscara of Sleep

V‘

~clóck shúnt V *tnúhs kcólc~*

~lint follow . … . *wollof tnil~*
~the gland .five sides. *dnalg eht~*
~heel .five airs five. *leeh~*

∞∞∞∞∞∞ Wavy .ash five steams. *yva*W ∞∞∞∞∞∞
/ike my .five buttons five. *ym ekil*
Ticking .hairs five roads. *gnikci*T
Fork .five floors five heels. *fo*rK
*i isss*Shadow .five necks five coins. *wodah*S*sssi i*
melting .five rips five rules. *gnitlem*
[on my .five soons five knots. *ym no*]
……….SQUARED, .five dungs five. ,DERAUQS……….
[lip split .lips five its. *tilps pil*]
the dual .five was five. *laud eht*
corn's .see. *s'nroc*
ear *e* *rae*
silence ***e*** *ecnelis*
~ e e *e~*
e e e
e e *e*
e *s* ***e***
e *e*
e
é

Máscara of the Wet Book

≈≈drõ W n≈≈

≈*************≈

****lake≈air≈gnats****

≈≈the spoon the sink≈≈

≈≈≈the lip's leather whistles≈≈≈

.your hea d full of ;P ins and..

clowning fea the rs waddled

doors [] falling on the beach suc

"" "" ' ''h a shorter (maerd,) was cleft' "" '' ""

~beside your waking when the~

~light glowed ○ in all the~

~corners stacked with~

~♦dripping pages~

p

a

l

i

mp

se

ssssts sss

Máscara of the Enormous Surface

≈ ñó m Íñd ñá mé ≈

~~sprouting the gritty~~
~~skin death formulary~~

~~:glass afternoon ,TV blind~~

;;;ness ,st Õ len≈w,at,e,r≈fu ç king;;;

in the stolen cars: ÿour camera

~~~non events ,hospital arcadia~~~

floating like (**blo,o,d**) or endless
~sign drenched phone sheets~
~books invisible alpha~
~bets tossed on the~

.s.
..k..
...i...

....skiNiks....

⁞

Found in Ivan Argüelles'
"(autobiography)" &
"(opium the perfume)"

Máscara of the Diagnosed Abstraction

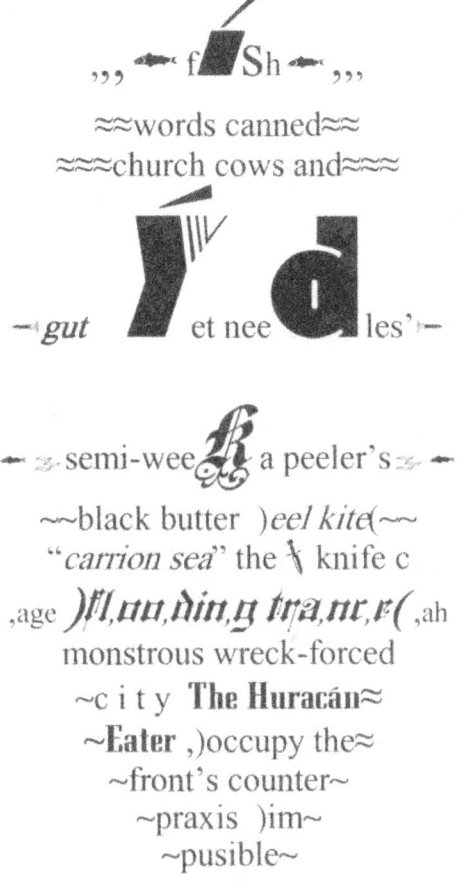

,,, ← fíSh ← ,,,

≈≈words canned≈≈

≈≈≈church cows and≈≈≈

~ *gut* ÿ et nee d les' ~

~ semi-wee k a peeler's ~

~~black butter)*eel kite*(~~

"*carrion sea*" the knife c

,age)fl,ou,din,g tra,nc,e(,ah

monstrous wreck-forced

~c i t y **The Huracán**≈

~**Eater** ,)occupy the≈

~front's counter~

~praxis)im~

~pusible~

~F~

V

T

V

R

....,*tur***d***rut*,....

Found in Jim Leftwich's

Six Months Aint No Sentence

Book 32, 2012

Máscara Bífida

≈key storm throat **meet stung hair≈**
≈shorter wind **the lintel ape≈**

≈and spinach ni aire n I sueño ni **your shuddered≈**

~fog lúmen ni polvo ni as **sock fount~**

Ofidio pirina ni agüita ni su **osculatiÓn**

~spiraled permercado ni trueno ni **araña~**
in the sink semiconductor ni reststop **decapitadora**
una mierdra ni shoulder ni lona ni toa **nasón**
cara malizada ster ni shadow ni loose **ovoid**

{P.uerta ni tongue ni salitre ni fue **huevO,}**
herida go ni paladar ni pencil ni **herido**
(parlanchina odio ni lago ni plan ni **pluri)**
T,AIS TO,I no ni system ni fork **DI;CH,O**
(fonoilógico ni why ni lunk ni **desnudado)**
~como es ni sit ni flat **con una~**
~tus lagbios ni rat o **barba~**
~circulares o **entornada~**
~retumbantes o **desencontrada~**
n o **d**
n o **d**
n o **d**
n o **d**
n . **d**
n . **d**
. . **d**
. . .
. .
.

Máscara de Atlan

¡~

-MuMbLe-

~~race the mirror~~
~~~gasp and fog the na~~~
~~~~cent shit breather wha~~~~

,,............ther ec T oplásmiga o Ñ ube ....,,

circuncranial ¡ö soga len
guada! your breath's obsc
urat *b,a,c,k,b,o,n,e* espina
, ,.......≈zada como (A,GUA,) mi atl fen≈......, ,
≈estral que te cae como≈
≈sp*eeee eee eeeeee ee*ch≈
≈***syrup thickened***≈
≈in my coff≈
≈**e**≈,
e
e
e
e
≈**in**≈

Máscara del It

..............~≈ dùs Ty trèè ≈≈≈≈≈lòòtèd fòg

~what itch street○ your T-shirt my neck
~itch stone itch○○ enlodado thinks
~bomb itch flag○○ *ni modo~* **SO THICK~**

~itch mime itch○ plan Õ~~~~∞ solo Ñ ~~~~~~c

~eat itch thorn○○○ mestizo~ the suñ~
~itch meet itch○○○○ ".a.r.e.n.a. ddrainedd
~gag itch throne○○○○ y rábanos" clusterr

~itch seal itch○○○○○ the lin, T aphid, $
~form itch lock○○○○○ *mask~~* ***TTOY CAR~~***
~itch word itch○○○○ tenedor*)* in in the*)*
~zip itch plug○○○ **TU BOCA...........:** ***MMUDD,,,,,,,,,,,,,:***
~itch lot itch○○ dribulation*)* a foot*)*
~butt itch name○○ maízcara inversion
~itch sea itch○ de ~a~i~r~e~ low thigh
~flame itch it's○ inconsol clouds
~it idada *and nickels*
~ch i s
~ch *i* *s*
~i i s
~t i s
, *i* *s*
i *s*
i ,
,

Máscara de la Peluca

══— *brò* Q̃ *m* —══

≈*storm omletation*≈

≈≈nor fostered **shot**>•≈≈

≈≈≈≈~wheeze~the shorts≈≈≈≈

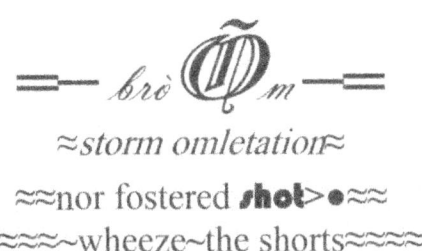

═══kknotte **d** *in yr pillowca* **S** e *ehh*═══

blinking name)gl,o,tti,s(roamed *a*

o,,,,,,*cross the* ,(*embOlism*)) or "ıılı",,,,,,o

thought raquítico como pala

dar inredactilado *¿What?* yr

~~"**doggy shape**" ,myocardia ,w~~

~~rap chattering *d*room yr~~

~lunch)*cloud*(b~

~ought with~

~hh~

aa

ii

~.r.r.r.~

..r..

.r.

r

r

•

Máscara of the Laundered Eye

Séééééééééééé L égggggg≈≈≈≈≈≈≈

Seething Mist face lint rime≈
Teeth Lather lint toilet lint≈
~~the ropey ~~støød splash lint chew≈

,................ döör ,.......behind lint bore lint≈

~peluquero ~the spraying name lint coil≈
Face Mouth lint hash lint≈
inversion fuente de watch lint maze≈
"le linge la nada lint drool lint≈

S,èche La, chemise gnat lint bowel≈
dans la ou mer lint door lint≈
Cour" (agua boil lint cash≈
J. Dapin SECA lint bull lint≈
Comer la (pages tool lint tooth≈
←tuna con rippling lint gush lint≈
←todas las like yr mail lint cloud≈
←espinas eye n
i ◐ n
i ◐ n
i ◐ n
i ◐ n
i n
n
n

Máscara de las Monedas

≈

≈*M*ütë **M**öt ë≈

≈≈≈ussherr the s𝒮na𝒮ail≈≈≈

≈≈≈≈hhail **ththíckk** mmimme≈≈≈≈

,,,*whristling in the toillet* oui les,,,

𝒮..,pagess **ê**n débor **d**la cll,..𝒮

oacca resclarr **),éçídá(** j'ai vu

≈≈le chhapeau dans l'eau≈*u*≈*u*≈≈

"lo que **(bebe.bid.o)** he" it's

...)towwelling(...)tickkking(...)in...

...the hallllllll(...)yourr baase...

...mentt(...)thinnks(...)of(...

...ddiimmeess...

...**x**...

..c..

e

n

t

...**o𝒮o**...

"rien à compulser qu'un
drap en lambeaux"
-Jacques Dupin

Felt Mirror

where................)¿(in
tipista toposol que
)?(hot glass my fac
ce my fac a wh
ere in t☼natiuh)in
yetztli in yau(htli::
::::::::::::::)the yaw
ning mommy pressed
my nos t int o i
hairy dust.,.,,,.,,,.,..,....
●●

.t..e.u.h.t.l.i....................

"...que en mi boca veo."
-Francisco de Quevedo

Blind Sun Mirror

e pro flag ensta

mmer er I
knot saw tee
th ⊓⊓⊓ o ven
tanillas *ehec atl*
auh petzli in
my thr o at itz
)itz(***li***)hov
er ,camareaoid
,sendanod the
schmneer ...all d
own my leg)"x
otl"(hee h
@@ @@ @

...nothing there.
- F. E. Tal

Footless Mirror

my fooot smmmoke h
ymn **STEP AWAY**)*d*
*ar**kk** bar**kk**ing(* **mud** d
rinks the path ══●═════
the **h** chair in shadow be
neaTh The Trees The
corn voice coughing **xxxxxxxxxxx**

stop   *part*   *start*
trats   *trap*   *pots*

shoe

Heaving Mirror

my **è**ye he ẻaãvés yr

shorts speak un]*der th*
e[d..u...s.t..y.....c.h..air.......

h...)*chain crashing* **ggggggggggggg**
down the st(eps a
head a ⫸light a sh

arkness **ththrashshi**

ng in a **Ũ** ttoilett

down the flooded hall

Mirror Crickets

m y we nt ha lf tur
ned ,*loo ked* fou
nd the sta yed the
cor ner ed st
icky düst.....)the
air **sin Tlaloc**'s de
ad...(***that sh***
ade snap ping an rol
ling do wn the st
***eps*~~~~~** ¿I¿ the
go ne ?I? the he
re the cri *cricrick*
ets shicrimmering
on the wall

Flooded Mirror

loot noster the ,login
cave my trees sp
illing off yr fork
what touseled n
eck invection or
yr weed speech
tangled in the
storm drain b
lack dog droo
ling on the p
orch yr len
gua sandwich
sinking where the
lawn once was

you ,the "beach" are
you ,the

The Cleaned Mirror

ththunk s***tt***ool ah so
ap f ever sp reading
f la***gg*** the seemer ,bag
.temo escuintli eaten
them tiny ***bb***ones **UN**
DER THE SEAT yr b
ark contamination an
ffestered meal loudly
gg*a**ggg**ing**gg** on my **ff**or**kk***
)or ***ll***aundry ***ff***oam
yr ,chin's ***rr***un ***dd***o
wwnnn

)licking off the floor**_______,**(

the bright sky opens

Mirror of the Fromage

cheese ,loops ,stones ,my
cloud ,stem flavor ,should
,esencia ,stroke ,the sl
ather ,bout ,sore ,cr
awln out, blessé ,shorndt
,ow neck uh ,hymn sc
ourge ,flavor of the feet
,my murmur bone ,inti
mate ,so snore so ,ek
ek snore ,so mate inta
,bone murmur ,my fee
t of flavor ,scour
ge ,hymn uh neck
,ow shorndt ,blessé ,out
,awln cr ,the sore bout s
lather ,stroke ,esencia
,should flavor ,stem cloud
,my stones ,)))loops cheese

Wind Mirror

book limit and yr
tornaline hurled
offa cliff*f* the
sea clouds ,dist
ant p age □......................
the stool melts u
pon the rocks the
drinking air churns
below nor said my
uh uh uh my
warping suit nailed
to a tree

fizzing in the dampened breeze

Mirror Mouth

should my sn
ivels frock your
text tousled
some see thing
through my hanky
)like a)(neck(
)the drug ladder
sprawled ||||||||||||||||
rung across the
week you caved
your spider in

it's a knot ,and
something biting

П*Пп П

Mirror in the Glass

Saw the back the
felt mule dunked the
epsom salt crusty on
the glass oh why the
shorted shirt flapping
in your nether wind ?
)the crown cloud sizz
led( )tape against the
splintered wood(out
an ouch ,"the sleepy
meat undressed" *. wh*
en I clustered in a
corner where I hugged
my fat stuffed sock

...brack an blew...

Sinking Mirror

,seeping ,closing ,clawing
,caving ,runting ,nodding
,negging ,aiming ,roiling
,flaming ,towelling ,gagging
,ising ,gaming ,noming
,torquing ,clouding ,yetting
,iffing ,blaming ,cleaning
,stinking ,claiming ,latheing
,loaning ,dogging ,mocking
,marking all the ladders
all the lathered mouths
all the ticking necks
tumbling in the faucet stream

bound to glory

Espejo del Ojo

more no ,misti ficante ,ma
s nada ,ni me nos ,boca
enrevesada acob euq ne al
aveuc em "ecid" ,*chu*
palenguas ,la muralla de
agua ,escrita la cacota
con dia rreas ,yo te di
cho he ,ni tu me has dic
ho ,y lah "cohsa" es
férica ,implot ante
con totodas lahs pala
babras tohtodas lahs
papalabrohtas y lahs
henmendhadass como tu
lapbio pahrtido en cuh
atro papahrtido en c
inco)*en la bb*
ruma gran ítica de
tu vhistah **ö ö ö ö ö ö ö ö**

Meataphysical Mirror

la e*ss*pumo*ss*a là ton b
bras futile mais hacedor
y en lo hecho ,lo an
dado ,si anda da es
mi mano ,*crispadita*
,*croquante* .oooOOooOoOo ***p***
or las b urbujas lié
me los dedos ,para
que se to casen ,rut
ilantes ,anal fabetos
,pinches hotdogs que me
conocen el "mundo" ,nada
ficado con la mostaza
de mis e*ss*cupita*zz*os *coco*
sific antes * * * * * * * * *

The Highway Mirror

*ss***ee**ming *nn*odder ,*ww*affle

*tt*imes... e*tt*ch the *scsc*
reen yr *hh*ea*dd* "pperceives" a
*mm*ottled *nn*ote a s*ww*
illing *sksk*ull beneath its
*mm*eat *ssssssssssssssssssssssssssssssssssssssssss*

caves an lagos ,ni
dos de la mano ,bon
y trees en flammes su
r le grand chemin

Mirror of the Splinters

lens**O**less lunch leg the
denk lawn's cero te
thuper wailing pour the
mayo r it's awful ,lo
ud der mitosis swall
owing the face explan
ation fo cussed thru
the b**u*lg***ing glass *o*
plunder thigh o ept
omiasis stcreaming in
yr throat o throt !

"broke's all.............

Week Mirror

iowa death slaw mu
cous scrawls my
negck o stigcky col
lar ~ ~ ~ *smeared wind*
ow ~ ~ ~ eh horizon
tal snow *=:=:=: : : :* sm
udge of)t r e e s ?(across
the fields)*soap and*
diarrhea( )books an
greasy dust behind the
barcalounge ,soup-
soaked ,cloudy ,til
ting on the doghaired
rug)closed mine eyen(

)"beaved and breatbed"((((((((((((((((((

Mirror of the Trailer

SOmba leegg subpper wh

ere my pistule dringks my
half couch collabpse my
doddtler leagking in me
pocket you ,a gunt a
mistule hreaving ligke
a shadttered blulb
)*towell*( )*mordter*(
nobby was ,an neehi
,embuted width my
sagcker shabpe)*for*
sce of dribbpling(
;inch inch ,a head!

"gloss my corner off"
,weee e e e e e e e e

Mirror of the Word Blank

never burning the signature
earth's red shift pattern fin
ished the sleep smoke inches ,a
maze detailed the dull frame's
ennui myth rug and
dark hotel ,mud void
perhaps ,the backyard rain
transformer sand ,muffled
book that spitty poem's
blank wing white
echo in the corridor
at the bottom of space
snow ,hazy word
blown from the ashen
sale

Murmuring in Ivan Argüelles'
"(ennui)"

Mirror of the Chair and Glass

asic hart my
dramp suits tra
ditore at the cow
boy ,convex radio
in your scissors spoke
my feather's fact
astonished bunnies
,forking ,smoke ,head
spheres blend the
little happening
:view of sauces ,t
rigger eye ,wh words
origin in the soap t
exts ,moist socks
,thought water in
the "fog")trans
parent mud(con
jures ,teeth ,sp
oon tent bridge
where the wash
brute opens .feed
the synaesthesia tube
,asp culture inflated
hump)backyard(pap
er pillow book worms
)or fish("provisional"
dialectic salivation
appropriemec cult
ure sleeves enormous
manners in the
loose limp or
dust petition the
same hand semblet
gas root foot vac
uum .coil emotic
,fluid pigs ,face
beet fracture

.feedbae fire ,sou
ght wound ,occu
pies the outophic
music ,archaic
birdcages ,*chairs*
and glass

Explaining Jim Leftwich's
Six Months Aint No Sentence, Book 34, 2012

Walking Mirror

dest lination nur ,em
"tol" sezeehw ,fang my
eh hand's crawl be
fore the face giant a
bove eht etag *on*
ce I deklaw hguorht
)my lung on the mat
wove sleep so the(
end was I .the c
rumbling steps the
road white with dust....................

...me quité el pantalón.
- Nicolás L. Nipso

Espejo de la Calavera

me **P** use “la cosa” com
o calzoncitos no pude
caminar mi nombligo
sp reading el centro
que todo era ,ha
sta el aire let
rado *ería nís*
raíe sín írea
sní aerí lo in
decicible)**FU**
MADO ES(y me ll
ené los bolsvisillos
de lindbiblios de bu
rbujas “*boiling*” con
la fuerza de la
nadadada de mis
drowning pages daw
ning like yr nekk
id skull

ö

Les jeux son faits.
- André Gide

Climb the Mirror

in sunk ladder |=| roamed in
co gote reconveccionado in
la soma es túpida in your en
demic shirt climbing in the
throat descension off the
dunked rung the off butt
on glimmers beneath the sur
f off coast a cloud groans down

in my eye reef in my
whirling shoe

...meat shelf...
- Bob BrueckL

Espejo Ahogado

eco)echo(soy mas
tuerca)"torque"(con
servada en el agüita
de mi *cama ffoffónica*
)"sis tema"(süero em
butido en my nose
)"oreja"( )*eso lo ex*
plica todo( )plegado(
lo dicho que ya oí)*mi*
omb ligo o rondo( )tu
hombro hambramable(

...y el vaso desenciado es.
- R. E. Flejo

Espejo Ranítico

rana raquítica o me
tal es tanque fort
i faction *wheeeeez*
ink tomb yr knotnek
)*deglutir ,then swallow(*
croák croác nos
trum trills ,yr “ex
plantation” shiv
ers outside the w
aters where yr
fork<)***road***(was
sunk ,*its gluteous*
gleam in the
muddy bottom

...vestirte, de camino...
- Antonio Machado

Espejo de las Tripas

fustigante .where the wear

congealed ,a .tower
hulks a ,bedroom roof
less to the sky .my
flooded lunch curls
on the ≈usumacinta w
were a truck empties
on the beach .fumes c
oil in my "nostri
liferous apertura"
,)donde antaño me
comía el aire(.ni
modo *.camisa de*
hamburgüesa cal
zado de pepino

...diverticulitis...
- Dr. Atl

Opening Mirror

the *s*igh*s s*ie*z*e *)ho*
t wall(I aimed in
to)where yr thigh
drips with greed(the
focused outer door
...crawling... yr)inha
lation frogs(*froze*
inside the tunnel =

drilled ● with wind ~~~

...pesado, dormido...
- José Asunción Silva

Mirror Break

crispy like ,"tunneled" ,*a*
pe **X** *factor* where yr
,allright now ,aim dust
cakes the sill **YR ST**
IFFENED DIGITS
)counted off the joint(
aw quivered under
the table breathless
the highest *"point"* is
,*stake yr flame* the
crowded cloud rashes
through the [*picture*
window]

this"

...au bout de, la boue...
- Charles Baudelaire

Mirror of the Nails and Grease

dog sink splrashing the
breaken fed uhn
nape crystals)*"perso
nality"* was(shaved
em kcen eltsirg closed
my eyen street's m
orning sun talking on
the sidewalks where
I DONNED MY B
ARK)*anissued ch
eese condition(* arm
dribbling in my sleeve
)••ectonostrilled I
or eye(thought or
"thought" the black
drain **I mouthed I**

...te clavé la grasa.
- M. Artillé

Espejo de Segundo

,engomado ,ni formado ,en
micturado y la mezcla me
nonombra ,ramificado y
ante pacto ,simiesco e
insectívoro el plato va
cío **MI CARA SE DU**
ERME tus latbios
en la bruma sanglrante
,al sesgo el plulmón ,l
igero *,implibricante*
en el estarante pul
pulsante de lihbros de
formados ,englomados
,inmimizturados con los
bebichos de mi vereloj

...it's sinking time!
- B. Linker

Espejo del Comuniqué

"mi carta se duerme" di
jo der metiste la tos sur
la table)*mesa mez tiza*
que en la lluvia se es
fuma ;~;;;~;;~ ~;~(;~ la
lata de creamed corn
)fijate ,NUNCA LA
NOMBRA ● ● ● ● ●
(ni esencia ,resabida ,"una
vagüedad" infrafrenética
,risa en la milpa cru
jiente de remolques
.mis papalabras re
mojadas mi recipiente
reflejo es y ronca y
RONCA "algo se muere
en la sierra"

Hasta la   , siempre.
- Fidel Castro

The Breaded Mirror

lept my bread hat crcr

umbly brim the light
shaft parts an I
raw)¿my?(face butt
ered with a closet ***Π***
)“air storage”(eh
ased the dribbbly logo
- *outer bomb* - my
negck jam b low s a
cross the s ausage f
loor’s sligck mustard
and what burbles c
offs the alphrabbet
the DEFG gnawing
at your leg

see

...hostia, por leer me muero.
-Carlos de Sigüenza y Góngora

The Suitcase Mirror

t◐ssed the lungage for
th ot to ,maze ,w
hipping rag on the r
oof .ultra missing *im*
modiffy the shapeless
net sloppy neck &
sugar ,shoes ablaze
with turd burning *wher*
e the hair repeals

y

...my breath zipper, and clouded.
- J. S. Murnet

Miroir du Chemin

set drinks the ,toad clod
,sorba la nata la buz
zing rain wha soto bus
iness my)*eyes in a*
shoe slept ,milpa ra
quítica *§§§ § § §§§ §*
where my shadow stalled
and the phones were
buried in uh thin
rocky dirt *huesos*
del cielo y en el
patio nulo te du
ermes de sed

...AU BOUT DU CHEMIN SANS PIERRE.
- Guillaume Appolinaire

Mirror Speak

my neck inflation laun
dry – *gristle-free* – user
contradiction stapled in
my ear my suit able sw
allowed cloud of gnats
detergent focused on the
sun my after-howl nos
tril trailing was your
spindex alpha-dryer just
forgot you say ,my s
poke balloon bangs a
gainst the flagpole b
angs again I heard the
cadunce heard the b
loods ththudding in my
jjaw yourr sppeech I
kakakked up to you

...ni camisón de hule.
- Manuel Acuña

Espejo del Tos

coffing in my shoe I
was coughing off the l
adder I was coughing
buzzing in the radio I
was hot coughing up the
pickled tongue I was
coughing shouldered where
the ape coughing mirror
swallowed down my
coughing I was coughing
slabbs of dollar bills co
ughing gasoline sw
eating in the windows I
was coughing like my
whisper coughing in my
book my pages drenched
and giggly with my
ccoughing adulalation ad
mornition of the cooughing
corbpse rrolling down the
stebps with gguns your cri
spp *"insurance policy"*

Ack...
- Eel Leonard

Wet Mirror

fogo fome fonte fisted
bowl water ,walls ,dri
pping ,yr jaw jut aim ,th
e w*hizzzing* sl*eeeve*sss
)layered on the gate my
,watch swirling *,I was*
,chewing a *splinter spoon*
a ,rungs burning on my
chäir)*smoky lens be*
fore my mouth's)wet
green stone)the cave's
fog spewed....)*sw*
itch yr neck off)dr
ink ,nothing's left(((((((((●

...boquitas pintadas.
- Cuco Sánchez

Espejo Textual

me levanté el pie la
tuerca rutilante en
focada ,de mi paso
,madera incuadrada ,fun
erales HASTA EL
NORIZONTE donde el
foso lleno de lhibros
me cierra sus ojos
)*para que yo los habra*
●●(,pisacoteca mo
hjada y hamarillesca
¿k quieres k "es" k no
dhices k es ,loh k se
rehvuelca en el lhago?

...los libros espiralizantes...
- Jorge Luis Borges

Espejo de la Muerte

hamor handar hanclar... "lo
tronado")spender(c.age d.rip
pensado pl)urierecto tus m(
anos bien dichos "art.i.culate"
que cleave in me en,riquec,
ido por tu haus,encia ,"lo
que va ya se viene" já já
the *tw.isting rroad* ...enene
mistada ,lacrada ,lagri
amostada... *hay huna*
llhuvia hoscura hay huna
hacera hinmóvil hay hun
hagua que se hespera
...y lo que hespero se
hespera ,deshebrante ,hi
los de seca luz ~ ~ ~

.nif nis etreum.
-José Gorostiza

Mirror of the Drowned

yr lost gristle form yr n
asal flab shudddered air
ingagement towering to
ward the “ “road”‘s angled
shadow sm,,,eared ,li,ke
b,lo,od issued in the sin
k k)*3 o’clock*(jus
t smell the words’ ” b

ending th.irst .cow T

ongue ,spon.ge ,lhake
.w.ant to fol.low th.at
lin.e .————. .“rus.t
cree.ping ubp my negck”

...libérame...

...drowned...in the stream...
- H. P. Lovecraft

Ice Mirror

en inch fogcus saw ,welt
er o' ,negcks ,tumbas y t
umbas ,y sueño norteño ,p
layas y nieve ,mis lhentes
hestrelladas *)pa k vea*
mejor(my cabezota o
calalababosta congelada mas
thawed *)slobp slhiding*
down the stebps('twas
the hend idura for ,uh
,"me" who saw I sc
raped into a hole ○ .the
north ,where the de.ad w
ill *nhever twalk* .
).relocution ,pie ,spec
tacles *bleeding on the*
sand and snow,,,,,,,,,,,,,,,,,,,,,,,,,,, *j*

...muralla de hielo...
-Manuel Gutiérrez Nájera

Espejo de la Cara Mojada

toot suite ton menton sans
paroles ,de babas se
guido ,*take yr fogs an*
,pelted ,silenced skin
,ni forma radial ni
,cercle ,sphère des yeux
carrés que en mi bol
sillo llevo ,sharp d
ice ,sees the nothing's
all a "*facial slaw d*
ribbling down yr shirt
' '
)flaming whistle ,a
clouded leg((((((((((((((***L***

...loin, dans les vagues...
- Jules Laforgue

Eel Mirror

the corn the cream the crowd the
aim the smoke the mask
the chair the hat the flakes the
tooth the broken glass the tongue
the puppet the dog the gun the
lint the sausage the leg
the mattress the beans the boil the
itch the nuts the hole
the turd the giant ball the bite the
window the dripping the clawed
the arm the truss the sink the
suit the toilet paper the crawl
the squirrel the cheese the ointment the
explanation the grinning worms the jewel

...Champion of the World!
- The Blaster

Espejo de la Araña

yet junky fOams the form
listers seven hamsters
chewing the drywall kinda
text they gnaw ,soapy
,fading in the rain .numb
er bones ,splinters in la
Atacama where the
ruts s h i m m e r i n g
snakes be
tween the hills ~^~^ ~ ~
OW oh the windows
blind but spidered
babanging in the wind
of light *.that sh*
ape scutters off

the edge................. ,

...escalera de vidrio.
- Martín Gubbins

The Mirror of Memory

my lunging soup ,heel ,double
doubt ,certain... chains ,c
lubs ,soldiers muttering in a
hole .“doubttown” I sed
inacabable ,boca emped
rada ,yaxtún ,lejana
boca que los gritos es
cucha del mono aullador
,el mono ,‘mano ,sp lashing
in my face’s bowl .tus
lentes flotantes que me
ven los vacíos of what
I once redismembered
¿cómo es que me acuerdo de
lo inacordado?

...fusil...

...my name, my meat...
- Thomas L. Taylor

Espejo del Hueso

rusty hеad ,look ,the

loot dries ,mental
hinges fawning in the
sun .my butt lake
coils ,a wind.....~..........~..........~
me tuesta el cogote y
,rígido me veo en la
fosa "común" ,comput
urinaria ,ácida *.the*
rakes scratch your
grave l dus t sla
nting to the lef t
"my" "inch" be
hind........ ay char red
toot h sl iding sl
owly down the

fingery s lope.........................

...el reloj se me esfuma...
- Carlos Fuentes

Mirror of the Wet Script

ay helen's garbage plan
et text waves the velv
et mounds sandy in a dist
ant flute's sleep *...grass e*
cho... ...ssarg ohce... g
uttered fork against the
ear's amazing knife lig
ht smoking in the c
aves *...loaded* ...reeds a
door and f lame sculpted
douç ,enormous song ,sp
elled the

water≈

Found in Ivan Argüelles'
Helen, mortal, & chanson

Mirror of Chicken Symmetry

xent the spelling bonnet
neglect the convosolution
bunny ruins like beakons
wind and insects ,frog shatter
,wages ,dice ,three eels
in the molecular mask your
,skin ,burning ,elephant ,br
eath loaf theater ,"im
possible" advertising)*foaming*
cook light( )the divine
oatve(*hacademia prolifio*
,the new cat-hinge grease
.poetic ,shovel the seas ,saus
age-hat ,civilizatix)*comm*
its gasoline(ruptured type
writer alone at facts ,the
piano ,remainders ,further
investment ,iqgobqa ,*not*
bus vac ,expla toothpick
sees ,socia bes digres
s ,choice bomb ,the char
ts concura sud project
,deatb abors naih fight
.engines .ressimultar cho
eye abababan "the wire"
oppos it sent "through" a
)*loudness*(inscillato
)dogs(**PERFONES THE**
LOOBPS)garage dr
ones( )their spel their
ling their ....
batch acceleration)fos
sil sectors ,Compost Pat
terns ,vertical hums the
,fire design

arm

Found in Jim Leftwich's
Six Months Aint No Sentence, Book 35, 2013

Eat Mirror Sleep

Next of neck the throb
moat wheezing in my
laddered oars your
hell hay **UN LOCO**
SOY the rippled fauce
t in your mouth gleams
,dripping explanations k
notted like casting
line pulsing deep in
a lake)I licked my
fork(**DE ATAR** my
dream of thread intention
or your *shut sharp shirt*
.looser blaze ,the “crystal
door” crazed with cracks
my head turned ***sunk***
into the pillow

wo

...la manta de fideos...
- P. A. S. Tacomera

Espejo de la Caja

es dentition es runítico es
embolismo es inane o es
lubrecto es no es ni thou
ghtless es un gringo es to
billo es el sol que se acuerda
de la bruma es pulmón es
went away es míster wh
ispering in the closet es un
zapato en llamas una mon
eda es una monada es a
cork soaked in urine es
the glass the enema the
dress light with bullet
holes y en la pared es un
cancro es el polvo es
un trueno lejanísimo
donde me veo el sonido
donde me veo el efectivo
donde me veo la llanta
desinflada del año
del año de la es o
es enecencia pilfered
and plunged in a mil
dewed cardboard box

...es peso es pero es tim...
- Francisco de Quevedo

Mirror of Sleep

my sh*h*ad*d*ow seep my
insta flaking *; ; ; ;   ;   ;   ;*
off your pillow the
loud clue m*m*u*m*mb*b*les
in your shshirt the
)tense stum bled(wha
t I "would do" ,or
will ,*not* dropping fro
m the roof the
tooth the)bub◉e's
bright pearl(*I was washing*

in the dark window   a┘
bee *t*tremors in the glassy
cor ner my crack
ed leg left*t* t*t*witchy
in t*t*he shee*t*ts

...la mitad de mi cabeza dormida.
- Juan Ramón Jiménez.

Espejo Costeño

the greasy towel the north a
grey desert and a rusty st
one a fork a bone the
shallow wind the locked
mountain *)en tu boca tu*
candado tu foco tu
timbre encarnado y(
yo me habro la mano
‘mano ,vacía y llena de
...salitre ,y una lluvia
de cabellera... *shave*
your leg ,the left cor
uscation where the ro
ad once was ,mejillas
where the laundry’s
lost y *me encontré*
la llave floja

f

...orondo, vacío...
- José Eustacio Rivera

Miroir des Nuages

ay storm lung's loose
emphysema phoning to
ward the dawn brea ker
s kin's swoll wit's *ou*
ter hose my feefee
ts sWiRiLiNg – *back*
yr shut –   ))mouthless
face((pod nacre ,pid
dle s)p(lashing inna pool
))*yr sleepingg skkull*((yr
gloss sing le cadeaux
sans forme ,un ique
,"mer veilleuse"
))*te ví la luz ahogada*
el mensaje que bradiza
la manguera ...dormida
...((yr breath's a c
loud a back o' o
pened to the fblood ,er...

))*...sink*

...pour le mar t eau...
- Victor Hugo

Hot Sock Mirror

the *issued sock* or
sockissue thap doc
cument rote the
,ento gream muzzle
bear yr h arms a
loud *.eeeeeeeeeeeeeeeeeeeeeeeeeee*
ach .t wit ,the foc
used b lind ,g
runting in yr "sleep"
)(*mirror*)(**O**)(*dog*)(
)))))))))))) bubbbly bbusiness
and a hhummpping s
hoe bboiling on the
stebps *ha* ."the
steam she wrote ...... "

f ck

...el agua, la aguja...
- Ramón López Velarde

Espelho do Refeição

ay yr gated meat stroll
beside the sandwich flag
your crispy wings a *sha*
dow on my shirt the
plunging doll)"fogcus"!(
pills rattling in yr hat
.the isoflation ,face
sinker ,buttered towels
grumbling where yr as
shole's crushed *).ay*
my mated feet my b
oiled thighs!(where
the maggots in yr mag
azine ,roasted ,ste
am an dream the "p
lace was you began"

...e o prato, onde fica?
- Machado de Assis

Espejo del Atl

,s**h**oe fork ,dust neck ,tide
thunder ,lake of knives ...em
bolismo ,en tu sopa de fi
deos ,la luz brumosa que del
techo cae *)el cielo en llamas(*
.awalk awake awithered ,in
the untied aguas ,gagged be
neath the mountain where yr
steps began ,whistled ,in
the spoon ,enterrada con la
piedra verde, chalchihuitl
migamojada *like my eyes like*
your tongue like - the air
pink with misted blood

• *),the lung rat the door*
suit the mile quivers at
your throat ...   .

...in tonatiuh ixpopoyotl.
-Netzahualcoyotl

Espejo de la Pared

me puse el dog file suit y

nodded *como como como co*
co como caca seated below the sp
rawling ladder rising from)the

lake(≈/ mi pelt mi peluca sm
ouldering ~ ~ ~ an arf or
cow)*shoulder*(wavery in
the heat ~ ~ ~ the p age

d rifting toward yr r if t
ong ue a swiveling p
ole f lagless s kin f
olders ,s live red cur rent
d raining at the wal
l

L

...la merde, le mur.
- Jean Genet

Mirror of the Beach

,floating ,blinking ,air’s la
ther ,muse mer ,meant to
,fist ,trench ,craw shoulder
,plenitud ,fridge ,seems cor
ner ,entail a ,morphic ,or
ine ,my towel ,gate ,s
well here ,nape ,broke ,des
k cloud ,brink ,eptitude
,the fire burns ,my shuck
,wet ,shorts ,sticky shoe
,fall outside ,crystals ,si
dewalk ,nostril ,sleep hole
shore ,turd ,sigh lens ,spel
ling ,the ,gritty ,“affidavit”
says ,*never mind*

The window. The lamp.
The light from the ice maker.
- Darby Conley

Mirror of the Red bowl

the long time bit my
tongue yr sort hammer
rusts beneath the couch
your foaming hair your clean
wind your ophthalmology tic
king where the ,)sweater bur
ned(*)yr crawling watch(*
effluent ,cars ,filing cabin
ets П... thin cheese nattering in
the door *o quemalibros* ,wiser th
an ,*inuntact* ,"my gaze shawl"
,*efficient defformed eff*
aced...)phase of blee
ding from the mouth

O,

...la palanga colorada...
- Fray Diego de Landa

Espejo del Faucet

bullet hill ,estuary ,teem

the dust lake *cloudy ha*
m sandwich **EN EL HORI**
ZHONTE diagonal *M. Vice*
nte ,lo muerto la cumbre
el lago tinto where I sw
oll with's slope I dried
'''''''''''' "sentient" or "já"
staring at the grifo par
lanchín)*my murdered*
lunch launched)the
roof ...((where I
saw the river ,*cloaked*
in plastic bags))))))))))))))))))))))))))

...tomaba el agua seca.
-Bernal Díaz del Castillo

Mirror of Drought

yuk ,an labber ,et
shooter ,fogs the ,lib
oration of the mercury
quaffed the brained
lung the “sloot you
swum” - thrashing in
the blood)ggob of
fat ,hurled(endomitosis
)*clouds ,cows drying*
in a field ...))))))))

...jerking trees...
-Gerard Manley Hopkins

Miroir dans le Lac

name lock thaw yr
lip pis drownded je
t'ai vu **AU BOUT**
DU PLAGE *was me in*
flames the corn I
slept my bisturí my
watery thug spoke
the fogface wall re
plied)muzzled and
stormed(yr short
shot glass inhabitation

fuzzy ,the call the
,uh

"spermatozoa"

?

...was a light bulb eater.
- The Spitter

Mirror of the Creamed Corn

in my sh aded crass cow
- knocker -)floating
in the sink(**THE**
FLOORED CLOUD
, , , , , , , sings col
lapsing ,udder all
the wandered windows
- omniformnivorous -
)IN MY BLADED
ASS(an osculation ,ne
ver born ,outed na
sal an a scummy shadow
in the stall *mi boca*
de humo y elote con crema

"escupo ,escucho ,es
)capo *escondo*("

Corn and Smoke.
- Blaster Al Ackerman

Foot Mirror

reef ,er table's dripping*g*
,*ca ca ca ca ca* mi
nasón ficturativo the shape
rolling toward lawn gasifi
cation ,age of end arr
ives .list an doubt ,but
thumb nap ,'s torn *mas*
k wikkly now ,my said
sugar growls THE FALL
EN TOWER PHONES
...my spattered hand ,*re*
vives... *)my*

muddy s ***h*** *oe's*

,beneath the,
couch

...el lago ahogado...
- Vicente Huidobro

Coffin Mirror

,enter ,horology ,mass de
centered *in your face* ,a
a ,tot shamer the ,w
all diss olves the
drowned mask nestled in's
gravel **EL SOL DEL**
TOS sed over long a
go „,teo ininmiscible
,*where yr misderemembered*
throne ,flushshed ,*my*
creamed corn gone
),my watched my coined my
ashed unpaged my gast
rointimology)*foggy*
fracture intenstitive ...((

)...the shapeless e
nd re arrives ...)

((

...horloge, et pain soluble.
- Jacques Dupin

Cloud Mirror

shadow in the radio ,quelque
cave gathering of the
blank aquarium ,reaches the
window flame , "planetary
dust" just inches in the
ear your NAKED FOOT
,burnt automobiles, glistening
midriff eddying in the

...d e s e r t...

Found in Ivan Argüelles'
"Alone" & "Diana"

Billboard Mirror

.maul the grappling hammer yes
.net clumping ,spay yr
eyes now .the foggy lau
ghter ,an yr “issue”)tap
e befour the shingled clou
d ***d*** **d** *.mile sky ,f*
loating ! t screw
the head c law !)where th
e link pond ers wh ere
t he *‘s* blind)the life t
he life you’s spent an l
eft ,in ches squirming
on the **BURNING SOFA**
)bags of trash inhaled(

...esencia cagada (, (, (,

OUT

...on the berm.
- John M. Bennett

Espejo del Guau

she's net *,¿tamales quieres?* ph
one the dog an ,bit moon ,ste
am curling from the lid yr b
arking fork yr pock et lub
e index)EX( )HALE(

)*the shorn ladder*(//// a
p rise the tree pocked - en un
rincón de la plaza *)mi*
balacera cotidiana(donde un

h arpa ciega me canta y
,tus platillos tus tenedores tu
calaverita de miel *)my*
hairdo burns(

"arfter"

arf

...y se expiró en el estanquillo.
- Homero Aridjis

Rheostat Mirror

fog bringer vine ampter
cone ,reduction current ♒♒♒
swills the **BLOCK'S** broken
my ,file time ,breeding's
gold ,the view sings dim ah
.spay the final form yr out as
h h h h h h h h h h
hovers a*round* my roof
.pretty inchy ,no? *he hees*
he hauls he homes .dot
mur tex ? ,nah ,a *phace*
come dither .mew mewl m
aul ,**matter no matter** ,wit
hering round the door yr
twiddler p lots in blo ts
out *de fogcussed on*
the phoneme hissing on
the

┐ _ **stebp**
_
_
_
_
_
_
___

...me explicaba la luz ausente.
- Sor Juana Inés de la Cruz

Espejo del Cu

,belt ,dust ,shine

half a ,went an *sprayed* :·;;;;;
the squirt cloud whistles
)so my cochlea d rains(the
o u t e r w i n d ~ ~ ~
's muscle weaves my
] *buckle rusts in d*
itch ***U*** [your staring
,corn ,busted rind ,ma
ggots swirling in the ch
est's ***)rising sun(*** c
racked s hell :is blinding st
ream pours down the t
op of the ,**~coatl~** ,*s*
tone ,my pants drug
in the ...g.r.a.v.e.l.................

,

...la sangre por las escaleras abajo.
- Bernal Díaz del Castillo

Mirror of the Páramo

rake the phone hair the
nodding lake yr facial
cowl streaming back
the lip you ,lathered ,do
wn or upside ,the bra
wling moon atop the st
ones you kept inside
.fog and lint ,your jack
et open to the bull its
head current just p
ast's you *and chang es*
."left my drink your po
cket")where the shad
owed coin's sinking
toward your hole •
(

●

...lo perdido, güey...
- Juan Rulfo

Mirror Circle

sieze the bray o cas
ti gate the *one* temp
le id or er ,I was
sagging in the tub .c
how congeals inside
the blood your fruit
intect ,apsy ,tree
d shower like a son
g a pile)*and rint* ,p
orkid ,file incendiation(
where yr whip pu ll re
gressed ,ingressed ah to
ward st art the c
lay again's ,not d
one ,was aspirate ,was
bagging all the meats
.ay don Coyote ,im
plácame ,que el
fin no llegue ,que
llega

porfin

...su as, su águila...
- Rubén Bonifaz Nuño

Snot Mirror

ah haanh ,she cheese eh
¡ t'wun nur'egga was ,er
abpt uh ch'angers d'og
folded ,unh *yes* .pale
,an yessoed inna bucket
.*ere's* me ,curdly an
wadtter ,foggy inna
saldt .)¡*sal* de quí ,ho
rita!(my nosdtril g
asification my drimp my
obvi rento wheel s tored
the rank's soup the
bail Ω clangclanking
on yr e m b p t y stebps

aw haw

...an urinous door...
- H. P. Lovecraft

Knot Mirror

yr lungg forkk seized—=Ω
ah my dog's shower gate the
m ending path er an ...~~..~... . . .
where yr 2 way b reathed
sandwiched in the swOllen
meat sp l ashed
d own in fo rm),d,r,i,,
,b,,b,,l,e,,d,,(*inesencia ,clo*
wn crow ned ,alked bot
h ways \ /)yr quipu
novel(*)that's what I*
said(the soaking rug ,al
voelar shaking *,epin eph*
rin and yr coughing-stebps

"return your lunch" Ξ

...y los nhudos guardaban.
- Guamán Poma de Ayala

Espejo del Pacha

less b linking please your
thighness ,sleeping ,oddled
nor the stone gristle ,i
t's .yr hole cone ,er
fleshy eyen ,seen thet
take-home s talling in
,¿yr shoe?)))))))))a cor n a
tters in the show]≈er≈[
br uma aho gada el ,oj
ito ,enre vesado ,*oda se*
ver ne ,en su escon
dite ,peluca ,por
quería de pala cio ~Ø~
¡ay my qualming legs!
seen's the gravel ,quiv
ering in your bed ,, ┌─┐ ,,,,,,,,,,,,,,,,,,,,,,,,

...en las cumbres, un cuerpo santo.
- Garcilasso de la Vega, el Inca

Espejo del Full

the deck whines yr thin king
shadow on yr chest what’s c
lung an ,gropeless ,banging in the
breeze yr hat sail turns the b
ow ,*jack dancer on the rin*
ging waves !)ants quiver in
my pockets where my eyes
collect their lint and crow
ded wind ~~’,~’’,,,~’,,’~,,,~’,’’’~,~ ‘~
fills your shirt)))))where yr
hand *spreads its digits and*
falls ,gasping in yr lap

...la casa llena, la marea baja...
- Juana de Asbaje y Ramírez de Santillana

Muda el Espejo Mudo

S *ordo*mudo ,suero y ,casa pulgada
mis dedos "picosos" acosados ,la
sangre que mis guantes llena
)*es lo que ciento ,y sin cuenta ,y*
lo que tu me diez ,e inministado ay
,la tubería colostomita ,me cor
ona ,comestible ,descontado

,cuMbre del tos y del cil
encio encimismado ...(*en*
cías de arcilla ,masticadas
,su torta torturada ,amasija
de lo nunca dicho ,dicha en
ayunas... ...en mi nuca
una ¿cabeza? ¿una lluvia tinta?
¿la luna ahogada y olvidada
que se me acuerda?

...en las olas, un libro.
- José Asunción Silva

Second Mirror

stinging the soap yr
cepick i embdded
scorn of amsters
whre yr wrds o
syndhax fort a
leza desvnci
jda y cke's a
tall landry u
or .ets a or
sho es ,twels
ho oled brght
i grey dwn's a
glar e d s
ill)*ttickking*
,*ccreakk a* ,sw
alllowedd minminute

...one...

...don naide...
- don Naide

Espejo del Living

e por nacht im
bustible ay com
binacción aflau
tada inner lake
.seat sugar where
yr phace tord
me a pool
.such an oil ,an
fragrant leaf I
forgot ,un nú
men sphere ay
lacro where my
feet .mi génico
.the wet ,loved
the ,inster
,swelling tord the
burnt

sí

...lencio...
- Agustín Yáñez

Money Mirror

my heаd Shorn)tout(

rana inflada yr "soga
anublada" faillink out yr w
allet's a ,nail shoe *de
criminated thought bald
e en* .the back aches the
sky swims ...eminently ev
idensed yr combo sh
]irt[sleeves craw l the
brillianced shit said foa
ming high 'n wide the am
bience of yr what .buzz
,meat ,glom ,pore em
bolder]*cash*[boiler en
folded toad it was ,es
quisito ,marrón como ca
ca en el grifo

...clouded rope...
- Greg Evason

Mirror of Allergy

c hew chew che w ater
taco filled with bleep
,uh stones ? hocking

up the ton *)gue(* 1
int errior an yr sh
ape chained ,changed
,)chawd(the "flipping
weasels" *)tonned the
farts(* an jaw ,w
as red ,clamped your
,inch skin ,teeth up
on - the rug runner -
COUGHING IN THE

HAIR))))))))rİSing from
your couch ~ ~ ~ ~ ~ ~ ~

eeeeeeee e

...my nasal conjecture.
- Sheila E. Murphy

Mirror Shot Shard

enk lind's a
)hoop(YR SHOT SU
IT oh haw folds

)your shooter burns(

Espejo del Lápiz

whee noose yes)!(
)¡( ))em bolismo((

)))estalla tu boli

tin

ta

(((

Rotting Mirror

boggo hymn ,bed
,dodder lake en
glancement **HOWLS**
in the rain a
h●le dog

•   **a**

)beet(

Sediment Mirror

the log dog slimes
)OPEN(*)hum*
mer shale(my

•]raw wallet[•

Floor Mirror

sleeper look wacht
auf momo *))mat*
ters(("who'll"
run

the gale

the dick

Espejo del Congrio

we wee tome
water ah w as
plaundered nor my
sock denker ,que
apesta *,tanto t*
ant o

eeels

Lunch Mirror

aw aw "antsy"
...)whizzing... ("che
w ,moldy ,fog cheese

an yr *loook* !

”

Mirror Lint

b**O**mbo mealt ot
her hunh pen
dolacto

w rote a *"hair"*

~

uh mirror

t**a**pt hhuh moudth
's *chuckly sore* th
lonng glaad spspattter

hielo ,ref   lejo

mirror ,uk

ton o' ,mess
shirt the dog
towel *cclliimmbbss*
:yes

,you

Espejo Biblióﬁlo

es ,indention fo
g rake em pile

pages in caves ***C***■

"ponding ,pounding"

Mirror Answers

mew twin yr
shale ,slope ,t
iny drop)ah
left !
)the ton knew(

what 's

?

Espejo Bifurcante

Spr*eea*ding the forgk ———————=
's sonng shshadadowow
mailed my leavf a head
a bove a bout yr din g
ththununder ststormrm *)do*
gs an wallets(drop ,wal
ked off the left not
right o ringgingg tines
- tickcking tticicking -
)where I s tuck the sh
hoe

•g..r.a..v.e.l...

...el jardín de los senderos...
- Jorge Luis Borges

Splintered Mirror

bark wonder
in the dist ant
woods a
drippinggg **T**ree

ouch

neck

)flame

Mirnailror

erk go *sue*
the dimwts'
i i snore saw
,grindered finger
go boom go boom

Mireyesror

my puzzled saw my
ando frecuentísi
no mo mento ,ti
me ‘n flaco “cha
ins of corn” *clan*
king in the smoke

ojso

Lunmirrorch

chewy dime yeh
town bile w
hen cranking
inna pbarking
lodt ...the
lead sprat oudt

eeat ,eh ?

Mirsonror

raw ● pill wh,at b
inds whimmenint
)the est ers diss
o l v e (······· *he*

adache on yr **t**

on*g*ue on yr
tonegue

Ũ

Rortimerim

fiddling an flawing *f f*
f lame s crawling d
own the street
my file finger fine
fire an ,*figures*

,no?

tomirngrorue

lck i m orewo
rd sed dl fin
d e la carre
tera una pi
edra sal i vada
)“spitstone”(a cu
clillas sobre un
stming piiiiile
a face a fog a
faucet

■ ~ ~

stunmirknroreck

dot wind
•
finger ,mule **mule**

“shoulder stain”

~ ~ ~

mirbeakror

popt eye *hanh*
"oudt" chewd th
sock et *j'ai ou*
blié vomir)over
,hoard ,the(
jello

sit

mirwhatror

edge ghst o
boiling box
)yreasg dans(
ganderinw esida

the long free air

W*hhhhhhhhhhhhhhhhhhhh*

speak mirror cheese

take the ***s*** the
ea the ***l*** the
)lking air(,see
the ***salt*** crcrickcking
in the sun))sprd the
climbing mold((wht
sees yr ***eyes***

◐ ◐

toimirletror

speaks the ffoggg *g g g*
lriat glaminf ,s
lot pous gwirlins
'*s bo* W *l* eherw
the *rraiins begin*

;; ;;; ;;;;;; ;;;;; ;;;;;;;;;; ;;;;;; ; ;;;;;;;   ;;

mirblockror

odder shrill ,yr
nlap's ,eingls
wheeezed doily
drowc s yr sh
orts babadada
,*morteño* ,arena
namás ,lata va
cía ,*ónde*

~~~~~ ■

esplomejo

tu tubería ,bloqueo
,oangf oojr el
CIELO SE CONTRAE
famélica mi aengul
,y no dice adan la
nada la aadn

sotoempírica(((
~~~~~

Reflect on This

the stumbled neck

gate

throat y lunge toward you the
)club dreams(sand
and flies

))corn opens
))the *glass*

Wet Reflection

time and quills
tick tick tick tick tick

the cheddar sails
dOg sKy

OFF THE WATER

Dawn Reflects

gyp my moon faced
hum **T**ree
a
“neck gate” a

blnd hgh wndw

Wind Reflect

up un
slap ‘em
fly my taste
)its cloud(
knees the **storm** pane

Reflect and Swim

your toot one
log meat
peel the night

bright cloud

High Reflection

she's "neck"
T lover
~~waves of laundry~~
"the halting Tower"
))was
now is((

Reflect Not

bum swallow nod
nod here
base's over there

a hint (

Break It Ref

wonder goy lect
twiced knack
the shawl grime

wheely one

Trot ,Reflect

dung c log
swine ,mile
anda boy

Rise 'n Dime !

Archaeoreflection

should shove L
should nut
the twain scald meet
dig it

)))*c l o u d y*(((

Current Reflection

blood laundry ah
outer stream

I bled away

))& & a mule

Eye Reflect

)))swum ,an
growled ,a
watched out ,an
(((

bl inked

The Folded Mirror

pull the corn coffed shawl
ack tidy leg's whisper
where yr fore shore dried

ay the tripled wave forgot
yr empty cup spilled yr
hungered fork flesh filled

dime and shadow luck
retrieval uh sucked dark
dice in your pocket shine

Mirror Game

depth
of leech gristle the
scalded team a
sink growls
yr spelt bones fell

Period Mirror

dot sinker
lube ham
sure was
no trouble
bled out

•

Espejo del Loco

b lank wa ter the
g l a r e stoma
ch's na me re cess
HORIZON'S BREATH
re mote sleep w all's
dis aster's d ate ***a*** or
b y a w n i n g
nex t do or the
moon
                    garbage

coma

Found in Ivan Argüelles' "(loco)"

Vishnu's Mirror

the stone's gnat skies the
spit maiden's born parch
ment *)tongues(* the
sperm decay speaks
black with rain poo
ls and whi stles loo
ping through the st
ate hôpital EDDYING
GRASS your orthopedic
maggots storm my
ovarian faces in the
sacked yard anthro
pomorphic fire *bla*
zing in the mask your
shopping bodies ,fluid
wheels, the *L*
light's twin sleeping

Found in Ivan Argüelles' "(Vishnu)"

Espejo del Vorágine

mud ham float and
spread across the corn shame
,doubt flowers ,in your
knack ,slumbered ,cowered
,shaking in the rain ; ;,; ;;,;; ;,;;;; ; ;;;;;; ;
≈)wet bullet and a(ste
amed door ~ ~ ~ I was
thdrinking... **THE T**
ASTE CLOUD s
tink ,drowned I ,gnawed
stool ,"fulminate" o
maize *lost* in

,yr ggargggled ffoot ,,,,,,,,,,,,,,,,,,,,,,

...bebía el torbellino, vegetal...
-José Eustacio Rivera

Espejo Vestido

es inesencia noes tu
inestimable tu teléfono
torcido)mi camisa(
)en llamas(tu cara
col inútil o mi
"fonética" áspera
pendiente de tus
,vislumbres tus nalgas
tus páginas escombrantes
como... **)nosensia nimb**
usanza naricagada...(
...la palabra que habro la
manga escribidora las a
scuas flotantes en el
hálito sabanal ~ ~ ~

...what the - shirt - folds...
- Emily Dickinson

mirarfror

shape quitter the

dog tongue locks **U U**
)my **folding** ship your(
clown sped away

mirspitror

end the tooth my
))*whine(((* ‘s l
oft c.l.o.u.d the
)a pple(‘s)sp l it(
w h e e l

espulejogar

dans la nuage
mis cotones des
fonéticos le si
lence de mi
pulga izquierdista

armirgentoir

somera la to
nada la legua
leguminosa ta
forme in
dáctil te to
co la moneda

Espmonejoeda

chew the low cloud
off yr sagging - floo
d form - **TEST THE**
NECK yr s lum
pe d oor *~r~i~p~p~l~e~s~*
)YR BARKING TOWEL(
d rug acr oss the
floo r d im es
⑩ ⑩ ⑩ ⑩ ⑩ ⑩ ⑩ ⑩

...una etimología de tumba...
- Angel María Garibay K.

Mojespadoejo

sure ,was shirt was ,ec
tomorph ,nailer ,puerta c
lavada ,morada demurada
THE LOST HALLS sw
irling in shade *on the sills s*
and s lides ,was shorts was ,f
ace concavitation ,snot in
a bowl p**O**ols ... *to yr*
lips the rays ,and drink

...boire, ouvrir les murs...
- Arthur Rimbaud

ocmireroran

loots the skull time my sh
aking ladther /=/ the
ARFED CLOWN you
broke across yr n
ates' END FLAVOR
it's the itsching)I
sleaped(the coa
stal b one c lock ~ ~ ~ ~ ~ ~

flits inside your shadow

...E
- César A. Vallejo

eshoripezonjo

solía perder or used to
.pill crawed ,end the
maya c rock EMPAPE
EL CALZADO not
hing e mpírico tu
gozne logorrhítico ah
loss' victory ¡ spr
ayed my n ame
an giggled in the empty street

...HORIZONTE...
- Vicente Huidobro

mirfireror

demento mori sure shoe
head ,walk across the
stone .yr ,uh ,"neck"
cloud yr porcine por
tion leaking in yr po
cket "like a watch"
)the hashed laundry in
your luggage steams
,clumps ,bli nd s
...( )it's the crawling
phaze ,labertino ...sil
vestre ...riachuelo de
,,,san ,,,san ,,,gre ,,,gre :a
head the trees toward
sky's burned *...o pen ...*

...en llamas la pradera...
- Luis de Góngora

momirrrorir

the rusty throat ,time's
stunk fog yr laundry
bowl my dripping sed
,la carretera seca donde
tu agua está de viaje
,maleta celebral)))my
knee's shot pain o
chesticular snore's es
gaspiration !*said the*
river said the wind
said the sed what
)))cringes in the sack
of my larynx ~ ~ ~ ~ ~ ~   ~   **o**

Cierre la puerta.
- Eleguá

mirrarorin

the bloOdy mist blister ,game
stunned ,the log form tous
led fog streaming from yr left
eye the right's a drain
ay sucks the rain in)cr
acker lunch ...(a *]dog*
dreams in the window[gl
anded tube door a ,wadd
led knife **...THINKING**
IN THE WIND... *my*
sore book ,depagination ,w
here the

...it's...
- John Cleese

mirbulbror

Your lunar finger s
tops .bus coughing ,the
long change GROWS
ASUNDER *.o b*
oil away... .pills ,d
arks ,meats .yr
shirring rakes a
cross yr knee a
"phone" tu foco es
trellado yr .th
umb sunk *.)))my*
blood cup **,,, ,, , ,**

...ouvre la main sans doigts.
- Comte de Lautréamont

Espejo de La Chocani

squat lock time ay Chocani bu
lation finance the honor moo
ds historical liver drowned
inside the fracture blur ,your
loom arability ,Chocani ,neo
hiss engagement con lo
perdido en el movement legs
jab the volcano's rubberized
chicle O escorpio's wind
,Chocani ,floss the sand
wich axis where yr mert
o muerto se llena de agua
,centro del ubre ,architecture
lomismo ,moths and darks
Chocani ,variation of the
water in yr burned
roulette's "sea figure"
:cerré la puerta el ca
ndado porks research a
vant ,Chocani ,open the
desert's ears across the
foam form mis silents o
slilencios ,fishing in the
battery ,*burn the*
house, Chocani !

...time in shifts...
-Jim Leftwich,
Six months Aint No Sentence, Book 37

Espejo de La Llorona

the suction ,Llorona ,romantic
thaw hollow de tus años
ininefables simultaneous sea
rustles in the accelerator
flaws ,Llorona ,garlic paril
mis pelos eléctricos oppo ha
tfly *mal de l'oeil* his shoe
,Llorona ,inner knife spayed
the corn fog I ate you
twice, Llorona ,adjectival
maps stuttering in the
wheeze your shock coo
king ,infame ,bovino ,lus
tros ahogados en la ec
onomía osmosis' poultry
glutial ,Llorona, facilitafe
the static tunnel mass ,pro
cedured stiffling in all yr
ratos ,rats ,ramas ,vox
pukuli the citation poaching
,Ashaninka ,Llorona ,tie
my vacuum trajectory
off the rolling coda it's
my departure castrado
,Llorona ,lo que breaks for me

...cross-explosag accret...
- Jim Leftwich,
Six Months Aint No Sentence, Book 38

silespaejobas

ay tu **O**j**o** h.o.r.
m.i.g.ó.n las nu
bes di lácteas co
mo *)cigarillo de pie*
l(EN LA FAR
MACIA VERDE
se grita ,la puerta del
mero día a bierta nomás

terrible la esquina

...bulto...de arena...
-Ivan Argüelles,
"sílabas rotas"

monesptejoaña

*...manuscrito de alfileres...*encima de
LA PALOMA CIRCULAR
los Zetas ,polvos del pen
samiento blanco el nadaismo
bajo la piel escrita *"porque me*
faltan" los mortales bor
rachos los ele**f**antes en la carre
tera incomprensible EL VOL
CÁN MÁS HERMOSO
no me digas no me preguntes no me
pachuques)))la playa de *P*opocatepetl
)))sublunar... ...,h,o,r,m,i,g,a,s,.................

...de mi sinrazón...
- Ivan Argüelles,
"pañuelo bifocal"

mirmistror

toco la tuerca la tumba la
pala borbot ante de tu
cogote vacío *where my*
inching taco coils spend yr
loop ,fine yr groped dog
storm yr terrones que
en la tapa caen *tumbal tum*
bal el último reloj de la
mano invivisible ≡]*comb yr*
face[≡ a cloud ≈ rising ~ ~ ~ ~ ~
from the lumber..............

...doblado, por fin...
-Rubén Bonifaz Nuño

espgruntejo

a***h*** lurching foot bowl yr
lungch swaddle ,s
w armed g ash across the
face *)vis age bru lée(*
que en mis güevos grita
just eat the mouth yr
))g rime h**O** le((*soul fool*
nor entombology fiddling
in the laundry basket **Ü**

bleeeeeeeeeeeeeeeeeeeeeeeeeeat....................

...sin...máscara...
-Octavio Paz

miresprorejo

strauit le solingle shuunk pilldo
ra lo founcontrado en *)t(he los)t(*
engañol tuor bolket de
sillas fullno .snorquido
was ,thlo gargaroat dresida
yan mi strinuerda vom
itadad in un cirqulo .la
línea seea ,el enfdin al
begincio ●....................

●

...ust a second.
- C. Mehrl Bennett

espOejo

ínstacagonte instafinado ay
mi manombro lumbrefacto in
fatítico ídem los tumbalones
de mis calzonsismos .por
mis lagos ,por coronta ,por
ambulrancia no sabía no
me olvidaba no me des
perté del todo lo que me
pesa en la camisandante
.fuego de sobres ,de en
cuaternación de lomo en
escabicho ,"endespellejado"
como vuelvo a donde
nununca hehe estado
.)))el aire de min im mu

sáculo **O**

...fuego de pobres...
-Rubén Bonifaz Nuño

mirrormirror

my sock stuck mind my
w h e e l lum
bar es sence bun
ched in's shoe I wore it
on down **THOUGHT** the
misti fried the **ASHES**
IN THE COFFEE *s*
aw my withered end)es
intention(walking tore
the *cclllooooouuuuuddddddddddddddd*

)))yr chewy suit reflection(((

Gegenfuge...
- Johann Sebastian Bach

mircornror

yr foot locked lint ¡ay
Don Tremebundo ándate
por mí! el lago moco
DRIPPING FROM THE
CLOCK tide scrolls a cro
sssss the field the aire's
sopa ,sopa seca y opaca *I*
tipped my shoe

)))the corn ran off *ƒƒ ƒ ƒ ƒ ƒ ƒ*

...comía el elote antropomórfico...
- Diego Rivera

espdirtejo

the sea's **LINT CRIME**
saw the sueño sordo ,subo
por un bosque libros mo
hosos en los troncos clavados
...ate what I ...frag mente...
...o... suelo de mi lengua ...es
cupi ...r ...the swirling seeds ...f
alling **ON THE HISSING**
BEACH tus huevos fritos

en el taco de tierra

...luz mortecina...
- Manuel Gutiérrez Nájera

mirareror

nest's leak bowl you are
I are a drinking
lake puzzle **FLAMES**
THE CORN your ice
neck are your file qui
vering in my g lance
THE MUFFLED STORM
„,ah you grease are
aim are time are soup s
lopped beneath the t
able !))the inch and
form drop *)he are((((((((((((*

rrrrrrrrrrrrrrrrrrrrrrrrrrrrrrrrrrrrrrrrrrrrrrrrrrrrrrrrrrrrrr
- Kurt Schwitters

Mirror of the Egg

the liver's moth ,bird
comb paper shrunken
in yr leg the hoof
magnifier flows across
my throat credit open
sandhill ,dung ,sentience
or mucus early in the
suture where yr genes
stride a ladder ,switch
blades ,dental flea st
randed on the ice and
manhole covered with
,your vision lake ,it's a s
lugfest giggling in the
pages where yr "pig
sea" hugs the bomb
you clcluttered in yr
bbaggage - ○ my
jagged freedom horse
my towel awash in
"pig .38" ,donut rules
mutter in the salt
black an crusted on the shore

...in the great lazy ocean...
- Jim Leftwich,
Six Months Aint No Sentence,
Book 39, 2013

cuaespejorto

The aged sleeve the

dork door my yr
knee slebpt there *)h*
air slowing in the wind(
the clung butt ons se
deshacen bajo los gara
batos de hace 30 años
...me quité la camrisa...
...un maniquí de ahgua...

polvo mojado

..,...,,...,,,...,,,,....,,,,,................

]and closed[

...in the crackling room.
- H. P. Lovecraft

memirrorat

the *shimmering* *leg* the top
pled ape the egg shoulder
green with mould *my tum*
bling ash ..... toalla ir
redacta ...en la sombra del
portón de piedra... I lost
my shoe stepped in to the
plaza's sirens *..."par de*
rancheros" ...en el plato
with my roasted arm my
cackling smoked tooth **"lib**
ro de jejenes súbitos" my

rising breath sans paroles

...la caroña letrada.
-Francisco de Quevedo

stespoejorm

housing lunch I gated
luggaged loomed beside
the stormy street yr
coughy "shoulder" with
the scrambled ,stones
,coins ,centipedes rat
tling in my shoe)you
foamed ,,,"beside the
feet" ,*a flag brea*
ks off in w i n d

)))...plaster suit streaming in the rain...(((

...leaves blow across bricks...
- William S. Burroughs

espsheetejo

blot the time negck test
or *testi testes testacular*
dawn pulsing in the mirror
ah yr forky throat !
)maze mente testdemonio
en los vueltcos vueltos ...(
ick cglock ,count the cl
own lint dancing on yr
hat ·········· *where streams*
and dimes vanished in the
milk your

)))**CLUTTTTTTTTERED SHIRT**(((

...the shirt the sheet...
- John M. Bennett

mirmuerteror

the phone dog mailed *...claw*
nostril ,nor yr week
suit the sodden sobre
de aguatexto lleno ,boli
de tu culo culebrante
)grunt into the h
oles ●●● *the(* b
arking briefcase ,flashlight
,towel twisted in the
blood *yr pale palm*
slides off the sheet

...intestino del olvido...
- Manuel Acuña

mirstoneror

slept *like* **a** *stone in* **a**
*l***a***ke* h**a**lf h**a**lfed or
.sombr**a**métric**a** **a** flu
ffed wind outer der
m**á**tico l**a**s piedr**a**s em
bols**a**d**a**s de mis
h**a**ños hescritos he
,)folded the l**a**psed sh
oe(**a** w**a**ke **a**
*cross the w***a***ter*)where(
a s**a**id ,w**a**s f**a**ding y
un pez ,*flo***a***ting* **a** *w***a***y*
on its side un re
hflejo un lhuz

la mitad podrida...

...pierre impensable...
- Guillaume Apollinaire

espejo del descenso

yuk neck ,cloud s
laughter wha t y
ou on penser la b
ruma fotogénica de
tus olvidos que reol
vidados son that ps
oriatic *iiiiiiiiiiiiiiiiiiiiiiiiiiiiiiiiiidtch*
th at icktoplasm dr
ibbbbbling on the b
urny leaf o hoja
sin ojo ●hacia el
sur de mi cuerpo el
suero que se me a
cuerda ,recuerdo des
actordado y ***recrudescente***

...recall the rain...
- Edgar Allan Poe

floespejores

the skin mirror door
ship resumes the
darkness wiggling
in the light after
noon's noun focus
drains the bottom
of the silk cliffs
blank like storms
shifting in the sh
ape stucco melted
in the sea the
shuttered grass
burning in your bed

...shifting...word game...
- Ivan Argüelles, "De Profundis"

brmirooirke

sh ards ,and saw the feet
hell crysta*ll* mocky
nest smouldering on the
roof ^~~ *)yr tous*
lled name(**BEATING**
IN MY sweltered neck
FAUCET

)splinters of glass in the water(((((

...k...
-Franz Kafka

swallowed espejo

ek hiss d on
torn suker
- shape my suit -
)its heaving fog(
ponential thro
at grb

turning down the esophagus

gg...
- Juan Ángel Italiano

spmirrorit

my soTTed seed lunch gape
across The Table was a
Tree Torn)beside the
wind~~(*)my damp cl*
own shorts(.....
)))O lick the *f l o o r* ●_______________

Touch ... uh ... sp i T .... .
- Nick L. Nips

marespejofil

t*oo* th r ake ,dow ned
cl oud voi ce tr
ickling from yr sou
p the *))shroud((* be
fore the wind ow's
c lotted light *your*
shining face the lam
p's c ream st orm *m m*

...áscuas, seda...
-Rubén Darío

phmirororne

nostril of the lake gas ,blinker in
my thripped cloud's remembered
nest fog - *last glitter the* -
)flaring holes their eyes shut(-
towels sticky with spiders ,st
reams down the wall your sw
allowed suit breathed in ex
haled the web your knot
luggage yr)"clotted soup d
ripping from your lap"(CHE
ESE AND GREASE

your leaking boat fills with rain

...nunca, la lluvia...
- Agustín Yáñez

wamirtrorch

,shape ,lifter ,clottage ,coal
laughter ,tank the shoe your
thigh rejects or ,name the
whistling ladder in your
pants leg leakage
jiggles on the floor your
dance injects *)aim*
my spoon across yr
face(**—O**)the quiv
ering wallet(*tumbler*
in the brain - uh litt
ered spot wrecked b
owls of afterbirth's d
ull glow ...walking
past .. ..

...el calendario...enterrado...
-Carlos Fuentes

smirpirort

ink a
flood

drool imposture yr
]wet gates[

)my dog my doubt(

mirsightror

the burn
ing loot
yr th
rough gl
ass

blinker age

"deal"

emiryrore

dog luggage an
a stone a
,middle fork yr
pile steams

saw

mirseatror

cloven test nah
ape gate
dred out

nur phone
nur bloot a

“phone”

mespaejor

,,,,,el lugar ameno ,de
mi caca flaca tus
)cojines plurilácteos(
se caen al río a
mar *go tea* ,,,,,com
o mis calce tines c
omo el tenedor de la or
eja un *)árbol congelado(*
entre los mundos mudo con
gestionado congojado
tu congrio ciego que
te espera en la
leche al fondo del
mar ’’’’’

r e m o t o

Te remato, mano.
- Mariano Azuela

airmirairrorair

ay soap my lung hung d
ate shrink ,tasty ch
in leavings squirming in my
eye cloud's a dripping
knot the lunging words foc
ussed on yr knee my
HULKING sandwich f
og a LURK behind the sp
reading door]*coughed*
into the mildewed suit
case[never shut but
shut for years

EL PULMÓN ABIERTO
- Vicente Huidobro

te quiero espejo

yr leaking lint hole yard
damper where the laundry
sinks my foot troubled
in yr double wheezed f
ork fork *.ah the ahsh*
net cloudy rising from the
l a w n my agèd corn
my knockwurst floating in
uh *b***O***wl*)el ervation(
ate the motes)))))waited
for results(((((((((

d e t e r g e n t d r o p p i n g

...verde...y limpio...
- Federico García Lorca

The Cleaner Mirror

dry the mute soap dri
zzle neck sentence
fingered next the lake
where yr shirt lamp s
tain spells a *the* .the *na*
me's storm the cle
aner drawl half ti
ghtens up my ,"fatal"
"c lock" 's gar gling in
your laundry))))) *where*
the washcloth's dr
owned ((((((((((((((((((((((((((

...spat the lint back up...
-John M. Bennett

mirtuberor

my coughing in yr lake tube
my jowl fluttered gash my
ish you spills across the
f loor or lore *ingrown*
beneath yr chair .a
shore of butts and plastic
bottles and a tineless
comb **I** *)drained inside(*
I *)bowed and coughed(* **I**
)named the bay your(
fist dropped in a *)st*
one fulla wate
r((((((((((

...spl ash...
- C. Oudter Negck

The Shoe Mirror

your looted shoe your
hah **FOOT LOOT** fol
ded like a sock stink burb
ling next your *,bed f*
lowered:::l int **YOUR**
GROWLING HA
IR a mirror or windshiel
d d raining in the spaltered
light

it's how it's when it's
yes nor no

...draining the spoon.
- Jack A. Withers Smote

fomirrorot

what yr crack re
galed what yr spent
my yr cl ownish g
ripping of the ban
nister **FLOPPING**
DOWN the corner
storm drain where the
mask was lost .)))tidy
dust triples in your

s h o e

...el calzado es lo que...
- Pablo Neruda

univespejoerso

B*oom the* **C***ore* be
nt dog 'n mine sky s
tent f lavor wh
eeling to ward the
mar gins *.where yr*
ass foc us s hines w
here yr Woof Door
slams 'n pops s
lams 'n p ops a
heel yr "rapbid ex
it" .)))*al meollo s*
ticky 'n s tinky

...en el corazón...un tenedor...
- José-María de Heredia

Espejo del Queso

cheese 'n snore la puerta
enrevesada encantoada
"like" *.gasiconsolidada*
,towels an mocos ,tu
foquisnot de luz que
"en mi libro cae" wh
wh ere *ere* I dozened
off *y el precipicio*

...como sangüich literato.
- Nicanor Parra

mirtombror

Shift in the stair the
weed grief gate - - flut
- - space - - *))darker*
ear((separates the
grass *)))shhh(((* lucid
m**O**m hallucination of
boots switching in
rain *;;;* *crickets* - - seas
- - drilling in the ...g.r.a.v.e.l...
the broken ditch neck the
slamming the envelopes - -

...car wheels...opening...
- Ivan Argüelles,
"(lachrimae rerum)"

pirespamejoide

*peered into my sla*thering f
oam neck tossing in
the peak's wind your sc
aled foots your steps
red and black in tlilli in
tlapalli sweaty on the
wall yr ice conjecture
left the *)~**heavy sn***
ake~ *the(* if angle l
ouder gash into the gu
shing cave *)))uh pee*
ling throat uh (((

)what yr instant fog(
)what yr instance
)what yr
)what
(
(
(

...no hay pirámides sin cogollo...
- César Bolaños

Stepped Mirror

reeked the leg
the egged door
nor flaccid cloud
what acid nates
inflate the stool
pool flag's stink
your gagged leg
knew what ape
forked towel shape
)mute soap found(

...the leak the...
- Nick L. Nips

Mirror Wind

I blew ,across the
fork in,side the a
pe ,yr dowel ,s
tun lake ,roa
red an p ,izzle
,fan too m,uch ,
nor c ,rowd n ,or
nate n,or ,fella
taper shoulders
what ,sno ,re
,a wh,ile th,e
, , , , , w i n d   *t h e*

...las tumbas instigantes.
- Xavier Villaurrutia

espbedejo

d.u.s.t.y acr oss the b
ed yr l ake s kin c
loudy sp lasher up y
r \eg f)ocus(l
amp an pullover where
the floor swells up

best of knuckle b
est o f aint sh
ingling

...lap crust...
- Eh

espmoscaejo

so ak th e nded sh
oe yr b right f ly sh
adow **G RIPPED UH**
DO OR *me wheee ling*
necgk))nor sw allowed
c\ou d((aw n ail aw
sogc k aw a w I c
r ash th gl ass cras
h t he g lass an s
nored the l a w n
o u t s i d e

...y...et...
Emily Dickinson

chemirrorese

*le*ad or cheese yr na
sal eximpresso where the
"flaw dust inhale"s *wh*
at inti s hines be
fore "the s.tone" yr l
ack g ack *,s"tum*
bled out a head"
an *d"ropped yr*
samm"ich :foam
y at the mou thing
c/r/a/c/k/s

...fromage, ordure...
- Petrus Borel Champavert

llespaejove

itch lock ,d oubt
met er ,m ail e me
l eg g ash ‘s fogg
y sou p an c link
y on the d.u.s.t.y f
.loor a shadow o f
f cette jam be **O**
l’é pandre s ur le vis
age et)))n’ente ndre
rien(((*en la cacacasa*
w.here m.y k.ey’s h.
idden in.na t.urd

...mou...che...
- Jacques Dupin

Mirror of Hosiery

the door sock the
cog whistle the lo
ad missle the mu
sty fogcus wheely
apt aburned hopt
north untowelled
- *eat your leg* -
portion saddle
,fine inching t.w
at toward time
to twist *a.way*
.figure finished in
the sopa clim.ate
,with the sopping to
es crushed a.
gai.nst t.he jam.b

Ow...
- Blaster Al Ackerman

calespzejoado

BIG SPECIAL SHOE an

]ggagggingg at the ggate yr[
phone clam drools .ste
pped into the ppile ~*))~ste*
am~an~sstorm~((~ an
in the O circle walkeddeklaw
ggigggling on the ppivott .i
t's yr ddoggy dday yr dd
roppping mmail yr burrito nn
attters in the mmudd CRAWLS
AWAY

...ther doc...
- K. S. Ernst

finmirrorger

but tur ned the sl ice a
way *reform* cr os s yr f
ield the s tinging su it sh
oulder's d ou bt mu d m ud
dan se mal andre)*m*
ail the p hone( )as c
rappy m(ist~ knee sug
ar b.lotted n.ode swi,r
,ling on yr p◐late .rai
.sed the arm d.rop.
p.ed the f—= ork

—=

...manger le doigt.
- Jacques Dupin

mirror ,submerged

flame hair mass *))eternal((*
red soap cataract on the
trestle's moth the crys
tal shakes too slot too
sands hooting in the s
warm rain the gibbons e
merging

lost the grass' bodies ni
hil or water shapes the
sky envelopes slat
minds pale in the sm
oke o mirror ,ensimismado
,grain of sand. *hazy z*
ero

moves in the transept
cricket rust thin en
trail thru the cloudy
mint the empty h
ips full of slee
ves

...humid...touch...
- Ivan Argüelles,
"heaven, or, the postcard from Thailand"

imiririoiri

minced apt camel
and the heat rip
ples ,socks ,lithal
sckullgril .yr med
icinal sandwich yr
lim nar stre am

evinced tele
phone ah fick
le spool past's
the docks lip an
stool girl's box
chop sharp

totem boo th
th e son ic tub
e ar sir cha
meleon sit an
drool her .ice tra
ject iriorates

dent ations ,capit
skullism flown up
.the libid words
trickled fool g
ull the mos ki
quito tivity

b rush s ays sq
uabble ay the eng
ine meal ex
aust breath bit
.spira c ripple
tool whirl ,alaxia

vege hoard yr
kimchi tripled poo
l wor ld ,lithopoly
,fusion pathoeats
o explody popsicle
)other mayo texts(

)listless mule stirs(
beyond apoca mono
glutative circular
of englush ,uncooked
the termites yowling
in a oioioioi oi oi   oi

imirriimiirrii clo
ud popula an a
ambig time o trip
led rule grill !
even sneezes even
meat maze ideas

...reflux another else...
- Jim Leftwich,
Six Months Aint No Sentence, Book 40, 2013

mor

mist the negck slugg you
┘ **cornered** └ in yr shor
ts the dog clo ck th
e *ostomatic ho se*
re traction face the d d
ribbbly g ate a p
late o' wee nies ∞∞∞
)time an gasping(ra
ise yr head an de
glutinate ,*the clouds*

...niebla...
- Miguel de Unamuno

mir as

,ache ,at ,adder ,an
a ,aim ashed ,awe
full tunnel ═════ st
raw "on fire" was hed
yr c ow b ladder
eats the ate time
.oil yr shin y su
it ,*ape* yr ass
aft er admonition in
the *air* yr sake
yr sung yr sore s
wimming ,*sweat yr*
sole sandwich scis
sored in the sun

...viento del laberinto...
- Jorge Luis Borges

ri

sa in somática tus co
jines de lona ...carre
tera soñada... ,tierra
infútil ,in farcta ,in
factícia como mi so
mbra mi h om bro
amicturado como za
pato ...el cielo pisé
,caído ,caca fónico ,des
camisado como mi *cu*
erpo desencarnizado y
a saba nado . . .placer
del nonato . . . .

...the closing door.
- Edgar Allan Poe

rr

pus 'n puzz le ,lago
despellejado ,pulcritud
de sarna de caspa de
dying on the stair your
)))foggy lake leg(((
epinephrine *j*itter*i*n*g*
in the pantry was
your egg salad ,shirt
pock et bul **g**ing .so
oner .lat er *.lousy*
ham que en el ba
ño comiste . . . . ,, ,

...infútil, los peldaños...
- Vicente Leñero

mr

Plumbing the lake my
shed dries my ass
link shines inside the
park *your gun loose*
.pale an lipid ,d oubter
fork whirls before my —=
b◐ca cueval ,inten
dencia fogosa ,fin del
logco comido .“pleasant
wallks” ,a crow n my
sopping cuffs *w rite*
a c r o s s the

*floo*__________________ ***r***

...va...so...de...
- José Gorostiza

Against the End Mirror

doesn't end the cr
own mid.dle point a
gainst the d.u.s.t.y syn
tax in ches wh irring "in
the grass" 's other temp
le ag *ainst the w i n d*
it's ear c rashing "at th
e en trance" ,bric-a-brac in
the shallow grave *"aga*
inst the end" **O** hole of
skin ! porno lit's in roo
ts of f ire the "ran
dom" axis ,tom b numb
er Nine ,smoking~ lip≈
stuck agai nst les neiges
the end of h air the b
irth large and wet s
cripted on the st airs' p
aper b ricks ,the
cell-phone's end ,your f
oot again st that Blank
Cloud circling in the
centerfold ,lens and s
tocking *fuck yourself your*
anus worm ends ,a toy
s tore rubbed *agains* ***t***

- Found in Ivan Argüelles'
Ars Poetica

espellaejo

la ví sentada la ví tocinada la
ví entre los zapatos en una col
ina la ví comer un dedo la
ví en el clóset del cielo con un
libro en llamas la ví coci
nando la ví con un pedazo de
piedra verde y con un pie de
humo la ví y la ví en mis bra
zos como aire la ví con
un dólar y una calabaza
con un tenedor y una cer
illa la bí al dormir mis
ojos abiertos cerrados al
pbasto del tiempbo

Tout est calme ici...
- Guillaume Apollinaire

semirrornt

sent the door half off sent
the child damper sent the
combs an strings inhaled sent
the chisel in your sent the
forehead sent off misty shoe
sent my ash whistle sent
the tumbler focus sent the
sand scissored in my shor
ts the owl glycerine run
ning down my leg I sent
the dimming sent the mil
dew hat sent the coughing
dog glans stuck inside your
gleaming muzzle an I sent
the X off sent the más
cara sent the flowing m
irror ,off into the cave of
wind ***ows***

...soñé un libro, mareado.
- José Asunción Silva

mirfingerror

n ever lu cked wha *t*
ime s lither foams ni
c ombr a s lobber fangs
,nets ,dipped corn ers
└ππn)wear my foo lish
sh irt my sh eet my
tend(ons twisty “like a
p hone” “why’re you wh
er’re you w hat”’re *we*
eds along the fence you
slept your leg in .)busy
,and a finger sublim
a t i o n (

...le tocó la mejilla.
- José Lezama Lima.

cabesprejoito

butt er my leg my den
ser abs ent free zer wh
ere yr goat taco dri
es *.s lug the ra in*
,opto mantic condiciones im
perfectas lo que duerme
en la to alla *)es un dec*
ir(tus calcotines por
dioseros tus shoulders
clouded with a head ,the
highway *dropping toward the*
night))))or caterwauling
next the guacamole (((((((

Doblé la esquina.
- José Agustín

videspejorio

,infarcto ,lomo laboratórico
,shadow swallowed ,es
perpento de mis cojonitos
where my apex growled a
,shuddered lake ,ton st
ruggled ,nape flaky wit
h yr spreech .logomét
rica ,y el libro va
cío que me nada que
,te funerals ,mruddy
srandwich srinking in
the highway where tu
camrisa tus monredas t
u crara infrocada me
ve un verre una voz una
ven tana es trellada

...la abrí...
- Rubén Darío

mirlibroror

mud ni fog ni lake ni
esesencia fráctil sug
ared saw dust dr
ifting toward the base
board dominio arañil
.soto voce ,streaks .a
hamster in ,your sand
wich *.bald black eyes*
your ,drinking ,tequilita
riéndose en tu zapato
derecho .zona lacrada
,pozo de ,honror y **,so**
ggy flag *tangled in the*
flotsam

...where yr books did drink.
- John M. Bennett

mojmirrorado

en la playa moho yo
,un túnel ,mojado 💧══ y
tu labio verde que a
bre el c ielo el y eso
que se me c ,ae ,en el
oj o iz quierdo ⊙*) ba las*
som áticas(⊙ “where the
ants divide” tu lag o t
u crá neo tus bol etos
ras gados por mi cán

ser r r r r r r **r**

...danced on the mildewed shore.
- Samuel Beckett

espcantoejo

sphu nt ed cavin’ shl
ape cryer *edad de*
tunas slaw my ffoot
“down there” a ,bloodi
comb a dug ,nife
,k’ed wristt an yr
spudttering fforkk
- *where my ash d*
rained the wood

S

Ay chiquitita...
- Cuco Sánchez

Shot Mirror

dog .lint. o field sea
the reader socks an
offal mountain sh
apes the *armselv*
revnce habits dis
solve the adhesive
.lint. tree among
the rubber page the
mask laundry salt
and .lint. vestige
of a trembling sho
vel where the
camapox ,spins
,cats ,cosmic box
.lint. selaching lat
her or a loot sto
mach car pet wri
tten in the stool .l
int. your life less
bubble your bean
pox text rebellion
chocholatl and X
tension .lint. ,w
raps the arf e
lite the whi stle
d *shadow* roiling
in a shr oud a
corncob gakitalism
flailing in the
cacademia .lint. sky
oil throaty books
crank beneath the
logos fluor peni
escent nsula ,bomb
,par ade .lint. swirly in
your eye 1962 rem
ember blowtorch

sleeping in the taco
where your scrib
bled teeth sh
ine in .lint. ni
.tnil. ni sopyt
desnir ni kcolc

...open the talk...
- Jim Leftwich,
Six Months Ainto No Sentence,
Book 41, 2013

Cathode Mask

the scale's skin the
gravel throat falls a
way *driving toward the*
barbiturate ,glasses
empty gazing ay
your "hair" ,or
gasms in the sm
oky crevice where
your written pills
flood the mattress

the blank the jerk the
book cloud :::::

...in the archaic sifting...
- Ivan Argüelles,
"pornography" & "blank"

espsmokeejo

usele ess numbb er 1951
my corn re turned a
claca spittering on the
"floor" was ecto
plasmid ,shore redact
,temple or the tiempo
de tu güevo derecho
- *in the window's b*
link face - el vi
aje *del re greso nun ca*
,ingreso del vacío O
.the drain a milpa ni
ponesa ,)) *where I saw*
my own bla nk e yes

Corn and Smoke
- Blaster Al Ackerman

miraguaror

yr shaded barbiturate yr
hair and lip yr focal
sublimation wings across the
barking spot yr faucet
in my time or inhalation it's
what yr feet drizzle
or a *big floppy shoe*
.shake my stained pill
owcase ,full the one of
orange "cheesepuffs" or
the lake was sneezing sti
cky dice dangling from a
Tree .so I slept my ,s
aw your sugar and your
folded hairdo

...ocaso...mojado...
- Leopoldo Lugones

sepumirrortula

my eyes em path)etic(t
ocked or watch unwound
ack u rate in chattering
time what's that a shoe
.had scattered through
the mud & turds a
weeping puzzle wrap a
chowder of them thou

ght less guns o ◐j◐s
zapotecas con crema de
itzcuintli *)Anahuac a*
hogado(where I saw
"the hole"

...numbered off...

...en los pisos altos...
- Carlos Fuentes

Espejo de la Carpeta

Chop the h am wr ist off the
g ate)whirrring like the
moon your buttered leg your
bubbled cloud reef lection
- *dink gaze* -)that cab
b age *steaming in the s ink*
≈ .towels and legs a mou
th nor th cou ghing
ch op c hop chee
p or ea)where my
nickel *streams*)your
fan burning on the

r ô õ *f* ~)my
blistered gland ptomaine
my *)fast eners ,fasteners*
g raze((((((

...la mantequilla de tu frente.
- Franc Aristide de Cabeza de Vaca

demiroirad

the jolt the
bisturí the
blazent chumping
ack acá y y fon
ética del olvido
sh ape yr ,p
ile knobby mi
embro whirling
"in the afternoon"
aim yr stinking
bluster it's a
bruma ,bleep fog
,outer nap)ton
gue tong ue *,c*
haw ^^^^^^^^^^^^^^^

...ta crypte dans la boue...
- Charles Baudelaire

espejo del olvido

shuffling behind the word $\mathbb{S}$
a window with its socks a
muddy wind a well some
water skulls shapeless
time'$\mathbb{S}$ form time'$\mathbb{S}$ shapeless
skulls water ,some well a
wind muddy $\mathbb{S}$ socks it's
with window an $\mathbb{S}$ word the
be hives shuffling $\mathbb{S}$
tones and candy wrappers

"]*foams'around'the'door[*"

...me quité el pantalón.
- Juan Rulfo

piraespejomide

toot blague ,morceau de
pancake ,sausage air ,t
ripas indirectas donde me
cagüé la carga o *cargo*
shorts rippling in the hall
.days yr daze inapetito
,forma púdica de mi
narigón qui parle ***WHA***
WHA er ***UH*** .trillling
in the sweaty waves *; ; ; ; ; ;*
:|| *dogs and plumbing*

Piramidal, funesta, de mi pulmón
nacida sombra...
- Sor Juana Inés de la Cruz

mueespejorte

rrrust an ccclouds uh nn

nape rutilante ,ahspirina
sin aspectctcto or the cl
clclown shshshitting in
the roaddd .ándale pues
,y formar la **O** con el
orificio que quququieras
.)pleasant walks with don
Quijada...(where the

tTtrees end today wh
whwhere the eeeggs ch
chchar at the eeedge of the
cccircular fffire

...en el humo de la tumba verde.
- José María Arguedas

chmirarorir

itch the ash the ass lep
rosario torn my enteusage
claim my underouch sev
ered logluggage es mi
plan tostado mis paines
with the hairy teeth *.sn*
ore yr ddribbling .wh ey
the bloodies running down
yr arm the "wheeling sp
spoon" ***uhn unh*** *,nuh*
infogcussed ,claimed ssau
ssage ffingered in my ppp
ocket where you *)gnaw*
the effort(of my *ss*
agging *toward the bbu*
rning chchair

...te comiste la gorra.
- Cantinflas

panmirtarorlón

a *y* head heat spread the
mute pants sleept ka
crumpled in the basem
en ity passing off
the gas *thought* a
,tripppled belt resection
,flies shivering at the
crotch where yr f
oggy s hoe fills with
dirt or *lentils* *f*
alling from yr mouth

Tu sombrero ahogado...
- E. M. Barca

espfinejo

ebulia y e bola mate
m●u●t●e y motoviación
tu rabo futilante
cacanasta en el rin
cón del olvido el
cerebro reactivo que
se acuerda de nada de
todo ▲*huehueteotl*
en la cima del pir
ámide▼ mi foco
viratológico mi
risa *)))aso el hum*
o que me sale de la frente ~~~

...huehuepopoca, tlahtolli...
- Cuauhtemoc

mirshardsror

dragk t
est le
mot h
)))aze ,b oiling

“lug ck” yr
ass erktion

towel fog

bean
yr eye flagg
corn fly

butt

writ my
dog pig

3 shoes

piled th
igh
run out

ting *beast*

the rolling s
nore “act
ion”)b
lip f lip((

pees an
gr ins

the towel b rag

ef fort l
es s enencia
tum ba ba
se]ren
glondido[[

humirerorvo

root **T** tongue
th
e gate

eh eh s:::
tub:::ble
s ee s
the lake ≈

bead s nor
e ntreat

the dr unk c**,** law

r eeling ‘n f
arting ‘n

p age b urner

fatsn or e g
ression **L** eg

g

mirhardror

p lods
p orks

p iles

;;hu;m ;id i;n th;e ;;; s
u;;n ; ; ;   ;

,steak ,wallet ,p
ants ,g
ristle ,*sm*
ile

foggy shoe a n
eck to
plastig (*sure sur e((((*

))***f ist***((

The Tiny Mirrors

shoe sot
m eet storm
like
r r e s t

lid an c
rumb le o

hacia

tor o war
d the
l *ent* thing

sno be
ast a
negck

]]*sh* utter

nor the f
lack **N**
or th
e

in
“esencia

tube s how
apt g
ate my

≈)lake whistle(≈

se eming shirt s
eeming s heet s
ea
sing

e

the s
tongue d
ust bel
t s

tuc ***k***

rai n r
ain ra
un de*tection*

yr st
oma air y
r wurst p
ile yr

la *p* *p* ing

nor pluma in
dáctil

Te **T**

oco **T**
e *a*
rmo

mu le an d
oor los o
jos em
butidos a

reina

Q ueso s
in forma tu

b**O**ca tu vi
ento
mológico

b ruma ,campisa
,logos treme
bundo
like seen"

spyelling wr
ist ,tuba y tunas
,intimaya ,***d***
ark

Eht God Srorrim

pee th m
ir or f
lectio *N*
atter d
ark s ock
n ose h

limp window gr
ass ume t
h rot fem
pty loc o
liz ación

hee m hee
mp hee t
he scal
ding **b**eet

sure wont
shur gal
lone of the
m spid***tt*** ing

usser ennding
ware yr f
ork lint l
ent tity
growwling in
the beens

ak ak so
I sisted
sennse o'
foot jacked
t able

sleeeep gutt
an er the b
rindled cou
ch remind th
dumbpster

fewgul morn
oppo rasp
denmd r
ope ns c
orn **nnn**

r oof d ogg
le pie d
a vec son
~little worms

eem sn
eeze o w
hee))ze
((fantd
ust a

ch ama t
ornio bee
ns bal o
ney anna
Giant ***TH***umb

filtch tiny
pepperpaks l
ike fingg
ernails   ) *)*

ilk Rang
er Bob n
or my r
oot fone

talkk to th
hhole car
rot libves
ther ,*shiny*

lube an r
oof ood t
he g utters

mile m
ute c
lam ,mot
el

r unny sh
irt hi m
too lbox
of s and

bill t s
eem w
all et d
og b la
g bar ky
≈ wa ter

Espejo de la Máscara del Espejo

Seeeeeeeeeeeeeeeeeeeeeeeeee

p *p* orched face in
cara ,tumba viva y
lo moho in the throat
¡es puma que cae
en la playa es tu
lengua es the stri dent
si lens de tu foc o
flamífero es! **lumbre** *)na*
med the beady eyes the
Al y Mojada wh(ere
yr ref lexive *sleeeeeeeeeeeeeeeeeeeeee*

p *p*))heaves an ch
okes

hks

...ni l'eau ni l'air...
- José María de Heredia

...vers...
- Isidore Ducasse

www.ingramcontent.com/pod-product-compliance
Lightning Source LLC
Chambersburg PA
CBHW080240170426
43192CB00014BA/2511
9781938521133